Making Sense of the NHS White Papers

Second edition

MARK BAKER

FOREWORD BY
CHRIS HAM

RADCLIFFE MEDICAL PRESS

Radcliffe Medical Press Ltd
18 Marcham Road, Abingdon, Oxon OX14 1AA

First edition 1998

British Library Cataloguing in Publication Data

A catalogue record for this book is available from the British Library.

ISBN 1 85775 460 3

Typeset by Acorn Bookwork, Salisbury, Wiltshire
Printed and bound by TJ International Ltd, Padstow, Cornwall

Contents

Part 3   The Health Improvement Programme

Part 4   Quality in the new NHS

Part 5   Primary care

Part 6   The future for the National Health Service

Foreword

The Labour government's plans for the future of the NHS and of public health signal both continuity and change. Continuity is evident in the willingness of the new government to borrow ideas from its predecessors where this suits its own purpose. Change is proposed in areas where Labour wishes to introduce its own thinking into the policy debate. The resulting 'third way' offers a synthesis of the old and the new.

Like the last major reforms to the NHS initiated by Margaret Thatcher in 1989, the government's plans have been sketched in broad outline and much of the detail is missing. This means that NHS staff have been busy pouring over the White Papers trying to interpret the government's intentions and reading between the lines to anticipate what might happen next. It is in this context that Mark Baker's summary of and commentary on the government's proposals should be read. As an experienced doctor and manager who has worked in a variety of senior roles, he is well placed to help readers make sense of what has been proposed and to work through the implications.

This book is at once a guide through the maze for those who are perplexed by the direction of travel and an initial exercise in anticipating the future. Professor Baker draws on his experience to identify the key elements in the policy documents that have been published and to offer a personal view on what they might mean in the longer term. While not everyone will agree with his analysis, it has the great merit of being written from a depth of understanding and experience of the issues. It therefore has a real feel of what life is like at the front line in a health service which often appears to be under siege. Professor Baker has an unusual capacity to relate government policy to what is happening on the ground, and to write about the wider implications in a way that can be understood by others. This book will not be the last analysis of New Labour and the NHS but like the first edition it offers a useful starting point for practitioners and students of health policy.

Chris Ham
Health Services Management Centre
University of Birmingham
July 1999

About the author

Mark Baker is Medical Director of North Yorkshire Health Authority, Honorary Visiting Professor at York University and Honorary Professor of Public Health at the University of Bradford.

Professor Baker has held senior posts in NHS management for almost 20 years and during the last decade has been a chief executive of a health authority and a first wave NHS trust, a regional director of research and development and a director of public health.

His principal NHS interests are in cancer and mental health. He chairs the Yorkshire Cancer Network and the Yorkshire Clinical Audit Committee. He has worked for the Health Advisory Service and was the Director of the NHS Research and Development Programme in mental health.

In addition to his NHS work, Professor Baker is Senior Policy Adviser to the Sainsbury Centre for Mental Health.

He is the author of several books, including *Research and Development for the NHS* (with Simon Kirk) and *Clinical Effectiveness and Primary Care* (with Simon Kirk and Neal Maskrey) published by Radcliffe Medical Press.

Part 1

Introduction

The crisis

The state of the NHS posed a daunting challenge to the new Labour Government following its success in the general election of May 1997. Not only was the NHS deeply insolvent – trust and health authority combined book deficits were estimated at up to £1 billion, although the NHS had a tradition for overstating its financial difficulties in the improbable belief that this would generate extra government funding – but the morale of staff was low, even by NHS standards, and health service targets such as reduced waiting times and guaranteed admission for emergencies were being missed in vain pursuit of financial balance, which was apparently the short-term priority. Indeed, the triad of responsibilities for health authorities and NHS trusts (financial balance, containing waiting times to within NHS Charter and lower local limits and guaranteeing local hospital care for emergencies) appeared, in many cases, to be beyond reach. It was clear to many observers that the hospital service had more beds than it could afford but not enough to meet demand. The internal market was generally perceived to have failed to deliver the benefits expected from markets, such as reduced costs, sensitivity to patients' needs and higher quality of care. Fuelled by the Patient's Charter, public expectations of the NHS were rising and were further heightened by the prospect of a Labour administration after 18 years in opposition. The result of the British general election on 1 May 1997 led to an immediate and almost universal rise in the 'feel good' factor, reflected in opinion polls, the financial markets and public sector (including NHS) staff (with a few notable exceptions affected by Labour proposals such as GP fundholders). Meeting the expectations of the public and of NHS staff was always going to prove a tall order for the new government.

The politicians

The prospects of definitive early action by the new government were probably somewhat hindered by the unexpected appointment of Frank Dobson as Secretary of State for Health. Although Mr Dobson had been an experienced and effective opposition health spokesman during the mid-1980s, he had not had contact with the NHS brief for a decade. The proposals of the Labour Party in opposition for the future of the NHS had to be reviewed in the context of a new political team and the severity of the pressures facing the NHS immediately after the election, which had been concealed during the unusually long election campaign. The manifesto promise of reducing waiting lists by 100 000 in the first year of the new parliament was hastily abandoned and was added to the growing list of pledges whose timescale had slipped from one year to five. Such was the acknowledgement of the difficulties facing ministers that it was even rumoured that Dobson had been given the job in the expectation of inevitable failure and that he would be sacrificed in the first cabinet reshuffle. An alternative rumour was that the shadow health spokesman during the run-up to the general election, Chris Smith, had been regarded as too keen on spending (and was therefore sent to the Department of Heritage, where he could spend lottery players' money rather than taxpayers' money) and only an Old Labour hand like Mr Dobson could deliver the pain that was necessary to restore reason to the NHS. However plausible, both of these hypotheses were no more than idle tittle tattle.

Mr Dobson's ministerial team comprised three ministers of state and an undersecretary, an upgrade for one of the junior members of the departmental team. Central to the agenda was Alan Milburn, a young, ambitious and intelligent MP who had the added quality of a partner who was a doctor (training in child and adolescent psychiatry at the time). Mr Milburn's main brief was NHS management and he was the principal mover behind structural NHS reform. Another member of the team, parliamentary undersecretary Paul Boateng, was also extremely able, literate and lucid. Unfortunately, he allowed his undoubted intellect to be overtaken by the bullying which some ministers adopt to impose change or opinion on a doubting audience. With the social services brief, always a politically sensitive role, this was particularly unfortunate for Mr Boateng, whose table-banging approach left him with few friends in the service by the time he moved on. The third minister in the House of Commons was Tessa Jowell, the nation's first Minister for Public Health. Charming, approachable and intelligent, Mrs Jowell was well liked but not particularly effective as a politician, unable to think on her feet and often appearing to be let down administratively by suboptimal management in her Department. The added embarrassment of her husband's previous involvement in the Formula One industry, dominated by tobacco advertisers, was also unhelpful to her position. In the House of Lords, the government was well served by Baroness Jay, daughter of former prime minister Lord Callaghan.

Within 20 months of the appointment of this team, only Mr Dobson and Mrs Jowell remained in place. The untimely resignations of Ron Davies and Peter Mandelson, both in strange circumstances, led to the promotion of Paul Boateng (to prisons) and Alan Milburn (promoted to the Cabinet as Chief Secretary to the Treasury) respectively. In the ensuing shuffles, Baroness Hayman became an able successor to Baroness Jay. John Hutton replaced Mr Boateng and John Denham took over Mr Milburn's brief. Both men were quieter and perhaps steelier individuals than their predecessors, with rather less centrist views and in less of a hurry to solve all the world's mysteries in a week, but also with an eye for detail rather than a strategic overview. Later changes saw Baroness Hayman replaced by Lord Hunt, a long time NHS bureaucrat, and the appointment of an additional junior minister, Gisella Stuart, with a 'soft' brief around health and social care joint working.

Funding

Early indications for NHS funding were encouraging. Responding to genuine fears of a winter crisis in hospitals, the government released an additional £300 million, secured from savings in other departments, to ease pressures on health and social services during the second half of 1997/98. Although a significant proportion of these funds did not find their way into England's hospitals, £159 million was allocated to local health and social services, equivalent to more than 1% extra for the autumn and winter period and enough to avoid the winter miseries experienced by services during the previous two years (the remainder went to the other countries in the UK and to underwrite an overspending on prescribing by GPs). This followed a statement from the Chancellor of the Exchequer offering additional resources for the NHS (and education) in 1998/99 by raiding the Treasury's contingency fund. Unfortunately, these gains were also partly illusory, as raised estimates of inflation and the hangover of phased 1997/98 pay awards granted by the previous government accounted for half of the additional funding. The government appeared to be clear that its priority was ensuring that emergencies were effectively treated in local hospitals and that other priorities (financial balance and waiting times) were of secondary importance. Later, either ministers had second thoughts or civil servants interpreted ministers' intentions less precisely; as a result, all the imperatives remained in place but it was intimated that managers were more likely to be sacked for failing to ensure that emergency demands were met. By January 1998, all three priorities had been restored as mandatory. Further additional funding of £50 million was found to protect hospital services in the most insolvent health authority areas, an action regarded in some quarters as rewarding failure. Nonetheless, it appeared that the government was serious about keeping the NHS afloat, recognised the need to invest additional real resources and was genuine about retaining a comprehensive service. Indeed, by February 1998, waiting lists had re-emerged as a suitable case for treatment and every likelihood of becoming the political bench mark for performance once again. Conversely, the phasing of the 1998/99 pay award for staff covered by pay review bodies suggested no significant relaxation in public sector pay or health service funding in general. It became clear that the priority for the NHS in 1998/99 was to eradicate its financial deficit so that the new money to be allocated thereafter delivered service benefits rather than merely reducing deficits. The NHS management community was no place for faint hearts.

On its election, based on a promise of no increase in income tax rates, the government announced a comprehensive review of all government spending. The intention was to see what could be diverted from less politically sensitive areas to the key populist election issues of health and education. Reporting in the summer of 1998, the Comprehensive Spending Review allocated an additional £21 billion to the NHS over the three years commencing April 1999 and also indicated general growth rates and allocations for the whole of the three-year period (up to the latest possible date of the next election). The euphoria which followed this announcement was short-lived when it became clear that the actual new money available to the NHS at the end of the three-year period was about half the famously quoted £21 billion and that half of that new money (£5 billion) was to be retained centrally in a so-called Modernisation Fund to ensure the delivery of the government's own priorities. The actual new and uncommitted resources for local services to invest was probably less than for some years. Furthermore, the government changed the rules for NHS financing so that it would no longer be possible to use underspends on capital to offset overspends on recurrent expenditure (e.g. on staff and drugs). As this was the means by which many trusts had remained solvent for several years, this started to have a major impact almost immediately, leading to many more trusts being insolvent in 1999/2000.

Policy

Most new governments reorganise the NHS. It is not that there is any evidence that such changes are desirable, necessary or successful, merely that it is within the power of government to take such action. Thus, in almost every field of endeavour, the new government issued proposals and/or legislation during its first six months, fuelled by the long years of opposition and by the comprehensive policy review undertaken after Tony Blair's election as leader of the Labour Party in 1994, after the untimely death of John Smith. Rapid action followed in education, transport and, especially, in public referenda and subsequent legislation for devolution to Scotland and Wales.

In the health service, however, we waited in vain for a prompt policy directive. Positive noises were made about public health, and the government's commitment to replace the internal market in the NHS was clearly signposted, as it had been before the election. The long-promised reduction in management costs (normally referred to by ministers as bureaucracy or red tape) duly arrived, but was little more intrusive than those cuts already agreed, plus a postponement of the next (eighth) wave of GP fundholding. The anticipated public health Green Paper, expected in November 1997, was postponed. However, due to a classic error of organisation, the launch meeting for chairs, chief executives and public health directors of health authorities went ahead on 17 November although ministers had nothing new to say. The massive faut pas of the Formula One exclusion from the proposed ban on tobacco advertising had seriously wounded the Public Health Minister, Tessa Jowell, shortly before this meeting. The Health Action Zone (HAZ) initiative, which should have followed the context-setting of the public health policy, was duly published first. It was against this background that the long awaited NHS White Paper was published in December 1997. The Green Paper on public health, *Our Healthier Nation*, was eventually published on 5 February 1998, presumably having been trashed at least once by 10 Downing Street, and having rather lost its place as the front end of government action on health. The government told us that *Our Healthier Nation* provides the front end for all its health strategies and that it set the scene for HAZs, the role and purpose of the NHS and the accountability of health authorities. However, it was published last and, while *The New NHS* is introduced by the Prime Minister, *Our Healthier Nation* is introduced by Health Ministers; the symbols are all wrong and the plot appeared to have been lost on the journey. These political symbols are in conflict with the pre-eminent role allegedly given to health of the community as the driver for healthcare.

A White Paper

It is alleged that the White Paper was leaked in October 1997 and apparently authoritative reports of its contents were published in several newspapers. A strange period followed, during which many civil servants assured NHS managers that the White Paper was completed and at the printers – and therefore by inference beyond amendment. Most senior civil servants claim to have written all or part of the White Paper and promises of its guaranteed publication by the end of the week or month (November) came from the very top of the office. Ministers went ballistic over the alleged 'leaks' and instituted a siege-like security at all Department of Health (DoH) offices, including NHS Executive Regional Offices, far tighter than during the height of terrorist campaigns in London. To seasoned observers, the whole charade was hilarious as it is generally assumed that most reliable leaks come from ministers' offices rather than from their staff. Although laughable, the siege mentality did affect the informal consultation on the government's ideas for reform, which should have been occurring at this time. As a result, for example, the dialogue with local authorities about their close involvement with NHS plans and the attendance of their representatives at health authority board meetings did not take place. There ensued a six-week interval during which we were assured that final touches were still being applied to the White Paper and some decisions had not yet been made. No one believed this. At last the great day came and all the pundits were proved wrong; the 'leaks' proved incomplete or inaccurate and it did appear that important changes had been introduced at a late stage, most particularly in terms of the future management of mental health and learning disabilities services. Another key element of the proposals, primary care groups (PCGs), were also missing from the leaked version, suggesting that they were as late an addition to the structures as GP fundholding had been to the *Working for Patients* reforms in the 1989 White Paper.

Most modern political statements are characterised by stunts and slogans. Stunts create the mirage of action to make a difference, while slogans are useful for electioneering. The title of the NHS White Paper, *The New NHS: modern, dependable*, is itself a slogan, with no attempt to define its precise meaning throughout the document, although the 'modernism' features in most of the subsequent documentation headed 'Modernising the NHS'. The White Paper is structured into ten chapters, each with a title, subheading and key themes, each of which is a freestanding slogan (Box 1.1). The whole text is supported by margin sound-bites which are themselves intended to summarise in short slogans the thrust of government policy (Box 1.2). These phrases in the margins tell almost the whole story; they are the words which best define the government's policies and priorities and may be the only bits of the document which were chosen by the politicians. I am, however, reliably informed that this White Paper had a much stronger input than usual from ministers and particularly the Minister of State, Alan Milburn (it is rumoured that the final version of *The New NHS* was completed on Mr Milburn's laptop computer). The level of this political involvement is both a strength and a weakness; a strength in terms of political leadership, understanding and commitment; a weakness in the event of the promotion of the admirable Mr Milburn in the winter of 1998/99, leaving his plans without parental political ownership within the DoH. Mr Denham proved content with his inheritance but he has a different political background to Mr Milburn, which has encouraged him to prefer small organisations to large. This will have a major impact on Mr Milburn's thoughts on the number and size of health authorities.

This style is not unusual and actually follows quite closely the manner of the previous government's White Paper for NHS reform,

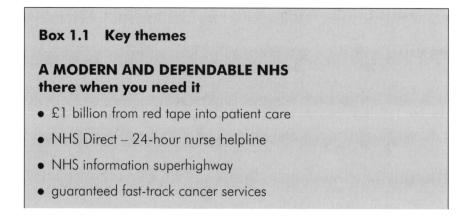

Box 1.1   Key themes

**A MODERN AND DEPENDABLE NHS
there when you need it**

- £1 billion from red tape into patient care

- NHS Direct – 24-hour nurse helpline

- NHS information superhighway

- guaranteed fast-track cancer services

A NEW START
what counts is what works

- the third way
- keeping what works
- discarding what has failed

DRIVING CHANGE IN THE NHS
quality and efficiency hand in hand

- raising quality standards
- increasing efficiency
- driving performance
- new roles and responsibilities

HEALTH AUTHORITIES
leading and shaping

- new focus on improving health
- new Health Improvement Programmes to shape local healthcare
- lead strategic role for local NHS

PRIMARY CARE GROUPS
going with the grain

- development of primary and community healthcare
- family doctors and community nurses in the lead
- a spectrum of opportunities beyond fundholding

NHS TRUSTS
partnership and performance

- new role helping plan local services
- responsible for operational management

- new statutory duties for quality and partnership

- new emphasis on staff involvement

THE NATIONAL DIMENSION
a one-nation NHS

- national leadership to support local development

- new National Institute for Clinical Excellence

- new Commission for Health Improvement

MEASURING PROGRESS
better every year

- new measures of NHS performance

- action to tackle unacceptable service variations

- new national survey of patient experience

HOW THE MONEY WILL FLOW
from red tape to patient care

- promoting quality and efficiency

- stable funding

- fair budgets

- £1 billion from bureaucracy

MAKING IT HAPPEN
rolling out change

- building on what works

- Health Action Zones to blaze the trail

- a rolling programme of development

Box 1.2   Marginal soundbites

A MODERN AND DEPENDABLE NHS

- prompt high-quality care
- integrated care based on partnership and driven by performance
- more investment and better technology
- NHS Direct, a new 24-hour telephone line staffed by nurses
- connecting every GP surgery and hospital to the NHS's own information superhighway
- everyone with suspected cancer will be able to see a specialist within two weeks
- tailoring the NHS to meet the needs of individual patients
- the health service is a strong and resilient organisation
- we are committed to increasing spending on the NHS in real terms every year
- the health of the economy depends on the health of the NHS

A NEW START

- a new model for a new century
- local doctors and nurses in the driving seat
- excellence guaranteed to all patients
- the needs of patients not the needs of institutions will be at the heart of the new NHS
- cooperation will replace competition
- best practice available to patients wherever they live

DRIVING CHANGE IN THE NHS

- raising standards and ensuring consistency
- a new statutory duty for quality

- management costs will be capped
- the pursuit of quality and efficiency must go together if the NHS is to deliver the best for patients
- leaner bodies with stronger powers (HAs)
- commissioning services (PCGs)
- providing services for patients (NHS trusts)
- giving a national lead (DoH)

HEALTH AUTHORITIES

- improving health and reducing inequalities
- they will act in partnership
- the first Health Improvement Programmes will be in place by April 1999
- more integrated health and social care services
- targets that are measurable, published and deliver year-on-year improvement
- communicating with local people and ensuring public involvement
- fewer authorities covering larger areas
- rewarding success

PRIMARY CARE GROUPS

- primary care groups will grow out of the range of commissioning models that have developed in recent years
- child health and rehabilitation services will particularly benefit
- the approach will be bottom-up and developmental
- primary care trusts running community health services
- deploying resources and savings to strengthen local services

- by cutting the number of commissioning bodies and scrapping both short-term contracts and individual case contracts, the new arrangements will also cut transaction costs and bureaucracy
- there will be accountability agreements between primary care groups and health authorities
- no barriers will be placed in the way of primary care groups which are making good progress
- devolved commissioning will go hand in hand with greater equity
- use their freedoms to improve primary and community care
- primary care groups are where the future lies for GP fundholders

NHS TRUSTS

- clear incentives available to help NHS trusts succeed
- retain full responsibility for operational management
- statutory duty for NHS trusts to work in partnership
- twin guarantee of consistency and responsiveness
- a new duty for the quality of care
- when performance is not up to scratch in NHS trusts there will be rapid investigation and, when necessary, intervention
- efficiency will be enhanced ... clinician-to-clinician partnership
- longer-term service agreements to allow any savings to be redeployed
- less bureaucracy and administration, but more good management
- a higher priority to human resource development
- flexible, family-friendly employment policies
- taskforce on improving the involvement of frontline staff
- greater involvement of clinical professionals

- the government will make NHS trusts more open and accountable

- no management information to be 'commercial in confidence' between NHS bodies

THE NATIONAL DIMENSION

- national drive to improve quality and performance

- the government will spread best practice and drive clinical and cost-effectiveness

- working with the professions to strengthen self-regulation

- patients will get greater consistency in the availability and quality of services right across the NHS

- new coherence and prominence to information about clinical and cost-effectiveness

- an independent guarantee that local systems to monitor, assure and improve clinical quality are in place

- the capacity for prompt and effective intervention

- Regional Offices will ensure local health services are working together to serve local people

- supporting and developing local leaders

- a more systematic approach to guarantee fair access

- clear quality control and assurance

- the NHS Executive will involve users and carers in its own work programme

MEASURING PROGRESS

- the way performance is measured and targets are set drives the way the NHS performs

- there will no longer be a narrow obsession with counting activity for the sake of it

- greater benchmarking of performance

- a new NHS charter

- the health service will measure itself against the aspirations and experience of its users

- first national survey will take place in 1998

HOW THE MONEY WILL FLOW

- NHS money will flow around the system to support quality and efficiency

- encourage real efficiency as a means to a fair and high-quality service

- raising spending on the NHS in real terms every year, with more of every pound going on patient care

- new mechanisms to distribute NHS cash more fairly

- the biggest new hospital building programme in the history of the NHS

- freed from the constraints imposed by artificially distinct budget headings

- the NHS will ensure that all patients have proper access to the medicines they need

- a stable framework based on longer-term relationships

- extra-contractual referal system will be abolished

- a programme which requires NHS trusts to publish and benchmark their costs on a consistent basis

- bearing down on costs to achieve best value

- this White Paper, by completing the abolition of the internal market, will release further resources from bureaucracy

- £1 billion will be freed up from bureaucracy for patient care

MAKING IT HAPPEN

- a clear direction for the NHS as a modern and dependable service

- the NHS getting better every year

- a rolling programme of modernisation

- Health Action Zones will blaze the trail

- an NHS that responds to a changed and changing world

Working for Patients. Like many previous reforms, *The New NHS* purports to support evolutionary change; indeed, the Labour Party, in the run up to the election, had made much of its desire to avoid major reorganisation. The NHS Chief Executive, Alan Langlands, was desperately keen to avoid the carnage and dysfunction of a wholesale restructuring which leads to most senior staff changing jobs. In practice, however, this White Paper heralds the most profound changes ever in the structure of the NHS. The government may well be as sincere as Mr Langlands in its desire not to impose dysfunctional change on NHS structures unnecessarily, but it underestimates the pace and enthusiasm of NHS managers when reorganisation is on the cards. The White Paper is also guilty of assuming that there is a structural solution to many of the problems faced by the NHS; an unfortunate falsehood for which Mr Milburn must be held responsible. Another proclaimed principle of the White Paper is the importance given to local views and bottom-up approaches. In practice, it is clear that this is a centralising government and that control of these changes in the NHS is being strongly driven and managed from above. Of course, all governments are centralising and, in recent history, each is more centralising than the last. There is, however, a desire to persuade the people that they are empowered, as shown in the devolution moves in Scotland and Wales and the elected mayor proposals for English cities. The government has created for itself a risky paradox of being both centralising and devolving at the same time. There are three sets of tensions in the approach to handling these paradoxes: the tension between vertical and lateral (horizontal) integration; between managed and entrepreneurial leadership; between prescription (national) and flexibility (local). The desired outcome of these tensions is a balance in which the best of all worlds results.

The structural proposals show how these tensions are being fought out within the DoH. The horizontal integrators have had their triumphs, particularly in the planning field (Health Improvement Programmes (HImPs) are multisector and multiagency integrated) and in community-based services (primary care trusts integrate primary care, community care and social care). The duty of partnership placed on NHS trusts, and their accountability to health authorities for implementing the HImP is a move in the direction of the vertical integration of local health services. The retention of primary care in the foreground is a victory for entrepreneurialism; the establishment of new national agencies to dictate how things are done (National Institute for Clinical Excellence (NICE) and National Service Frameworks (NSFs)) and to ensure that they are done (Commission for Health Improvement (CHI)) are prescriptive and centralising moves while the ideas for HAZs place a set of new opportunities in the local setting.

What is it for?

The government decided at an early stage in its life against a wholesale restructuring of the public sector. It remains a possibility that later local government reform will lead to a realignment of health and social care at a strategic and funding level but the political backlash locally makes it too difficult and unpopular to deliver now, and probably ever. Consequently, the benefits of wholesale integration of services to people, which are at the heart of the government's aspirations, will have to be secured in a different way, principally through local integration of planning (through HImPs and encouraged by issuing joint National Priorities Guidance for health and social services in 1998) and by pulling community-based services together via local primary care-led organisations.

While the headlines emerging from the White Paper focused on replacing the NHS internal market, merely a bureaucratic system for deciding how the money passes through the structure to where the costs are borne, it is the benefits for patients which should be the driving force. The government needs to decide what outcomes it seeks for users of its services and then to develop the structures and policies to deliver them. The benefits the White Paper theoretically offers, sometimes indirectly, to patients are summarised in Box 1.3.

Box 1.3   Benefits for patients from *The New NHS*

- Better care for patients by integrating primary and community care and, perhaps, social care

- Releasing resources from hospital services by reducing variations in practice and thereby increasing efficiency, enabling waiting lists to be reduced

- Improving outcomes for patients by improving the effectiveness of clinical care, making health professionals more accountable for their clinical decisions

- Enhanced empowerment of patients, through easier access to information

---

The principal thrust of the whole document, and much else in the government's approach to health and social care, is the integration of care outside hospital, and between the community and hospital settings, despite all the obstacles. There is little doubt that there is much to gain by bringing together health and social services in the home. The biggest obstacles have been the political boundary between local government (which runs social services) and central government (which runs the NHS) and the imbalance in power of the various provider professions. It is an ambitious aspiration to achieve integration despite these. There remains a degree of uncertainty about whether the intended approach is to integrate commissioning of services or to integrate provision of care; since only the latter benefits patients, it should be the priority, although it is more difficult to achieve, being reliant on cultural change rather than structural manipulation.

Funding or efficiency?

The government has dismissed the idea that the NHS can only survive in its present form if it receives additional funding on a scale which would necessitate tax increases, although it is clear that much of the additional funding on public services during this parliament is enabled by increases in less visible taxes, such as increases in stamp duty and the taxing of pension scheme investments. It also rejects the possibility of formally restricting the scope of the NHS so that it ceases to be effectively comprehensive, although the government's approach to new drugs such as the anti-impotence treatment Viagra (sildenafil) suggests an unexpectedly hawkish approach to this traditional perceived 'Tory' threat.

These attitudes conflict with the feelings of most who work in the NHS and social services and those feelings find sympathy with some members of the public. The evidence must have been overwhelming to persuade ministers to adopt a line which is so at odds with professional and public opinion. In the event, ministers have been persuaded that there is sufficient waste of resources in the hospital service to resource the existing shortfall and to improve services. The evidence to support this approach relies on observed variations in efficiency and the assumption that these variations can be eradicated in a way that releases resources. There is a precedent for this in the steep rise in day surgery and a subsequent narrowing of the variation in performance between trusts. However, this strategy has two basic flaws: first, it will only free up resources if it leads to major bed closures, never the most popular move politically; second, there are steeply rising pressures on hospital beds from rising emergency admissions and rising expectations. Only by closing beds, and maybe hospitals, can sufficient resources be released to legitimise the government's policy, and the government has subsequently placed an effective moratorium on further significant bed closures. Of course, the NHS is receiving extra funds, but at present it looks as though they will be barely enough to keep the service afloat, due to a steep rise in NHS inflation created by government decisions on pay, treatment of blood, use of recombinant blood products, social chapter effects (limitation on working hours), national insurance changes, capital charges indexation, etc.

Effectiveness too

The most ambitious, interesting and, probably, enduring strategy is in pursuit of effective clinical care and the emerging cloak of accountability for doctors and other health professionals under the title of 'clinical governance.' Both in this White Paper and in the Green and White Papers *Our Healthier Nation*, effective healthcare is seen as the holy grail which everyone must pursue. This probably does the field a disservice in exaggerating its potential. There is no doubt that much can be achieved for patients by increasing the effectiveness of clinical care, but the lack of robust and reliable evidence for so many procedures and interventions will not reduce public and professional clamour for treatment regardless of the lack of evidence of effectiveness. Indeed, unconventional, and unproven, therapies and remedies are the fastest growing areas of healthcare.

The year 1998 probably saw an irreversible change in the accountability of the medical profession and the public's belief in it. Revelations about service failures in national screening programmes, in radiotherapy units and in paediatric cardiac surgery in Bristol, together with mistrust of the General Medical Council (GMC) and, generally, of scientific advice on issues such as the transmission of bovine spongiform encephalopathy and the use of genetically modified food, have reduced public confidence in the professions and in science generally. The government's main agenda concerns the restoration of public confidence in the NHS, but lack of confidence in the professions is indivisible from healthcare so it is in the political interests of the government to raise the standards of professional practice in order to avoid public service failures. It is also, of course, in the interests of patients.

Inequalities in health

The last Labour government established an inquiry into inequalities in health, chaired by Sir Douglas Black. The report of that inquiry, completed in 1980, constitutes one of the clearest demonstrations of the impact of poverty and disadvantage on health. It had the misfortune to be presented to a government of a different hue to that which commissioned it and it was effectively shelved – although the authors' private publication became a best seller. On their election, the present government commissioned the former Chief Medical Officer, Sir Donald Acheson, to revisit the field of inequalities. This pleased the traditional supporters of the Labour Party who see this area as one which is truly theirs. The ensuing report, while published, was not circulated widely by the government, although a summary of the findings was available on the DoH website – a mechanism for distribution which has been used increasingly. Arguments raged within the epidemiological community about the legitimacy of the evidence and its interpretation and it was to be left to the White Paper on public health (*Saving Lives: Our Healthier Nation*) to apply the knowledge and the principles of action to reduce inequalities. Acheson's report had the hallmark of traditional socialism, hence the relative coolness with which it was received by Downing Street and the lack of early passion behind its implementation. The evidence that any action can reduce inequalities at local level, as required by government targets, is flimsy. The use of local frameworks to encourage combined action by health and local government agencies, such as HAZs, is a structural response to what is a cultural problem with cycles of progressive deprivation. However, intervention has to start somewhere, and the integration of education and training, economic development and specific health action in local communities makes as much sense as any other strategy.

Competition, regulation and accountability

There is an interesting perspective on the growing management accountability being placed on managers and clinicians in this White Paper. In many respects, the NHS is becoming a regulated industry, like the former privatised utilities. Experience in most countries suggests that regulation does not work in terms of securing better services for consumers. In the UK, a combination of competition and the naming and shaming of poor performers appears to offer some advantage to customers in terms of quality of service and cost reductions and this government has been exceptionally keen to name and shame in its early dealings, for example in education and financial services. Competition has not worked too well in the NHS, probably due to the inflexibility of most services; it was not surprising therefore that the government chose to adopt a name and shame strategy starting with the publication of hospital reference (comparative average) costs and death rates. We all know that the data are rubbish, but it will start people thinking about their outcomes and will, if nothing else, lead to the production of better and more reliable data in due course. In any case, high value-added benefits, such as improving services, are more likely to arise through collaboration rather than audit, that is through internal mechanisms not external control. Overseas observers describe regulated organisations in the UK as behaving like victims. I suspect that doctors and other health professionals in Britain will not submit to victimisation and will fight this type of regulation all the way.

The responsibilities of government should be restricted to two aspects. First, the government is responsible for protecting the public from avoidable hazards, including themselves; second, it must regulate the provision of healthcare to ensure that people enjoy fair and equal access to healthcare of a high and even quality. It is not necessary for the state to own and manage healthcare delivery; it does not do so for primary care and it has failed to adequately maintain and renew its estate in hospital care.

The management responsibilities of providers of healthcare are to deliver quality and efficiency. In the NHS, the government should be the regulator and the twin goals of quality and efficiency should be delivered through a competitive market, not the half-baked fudge game played by the NHS through most of the 1990s. The evidence suggests that contestability will not work and that only genuine and guaranteed threats to managers' tenure, such as that backing up the waiting list initiative, will deliver the changes required. That is what a truly competitive market would offer, not with the closure of services but with the replacement of failing managers and clinicians as the sanction.

The government has recently proposed the conversion of the Post Office to a state-owned plc. There are important parallels here for hospitals in order to facilitate new investment (Private Finance

Initiative (PFI) having failed to do so) and to encourage competition. However, what a competitive market and separate regulation will not deliver is also close to the government's soul, namely partnership in public services.

Working together

Another fundamental principle of the White Paper is the end of confrontation and the recreation of a NHS family with unified planning systems, including social services and the public. Having spent most of the last decade persuading NHS staff to behave competitively, it cannot be realistic to expect collectivism to emerge suddenly among health managers and the professions nor for the new approach to receive universal acclaim. Of the existing players in the NHS market, only health authorities can have any reasonable claim to behave collaboratively and I know of many trusts who would dispute that. Trusts and GPs are naturally competitive and members of trust boards were appointed specifically to promote competitiveness and to gain a march on each other and on their purchasers. This was not fertile territory for the rebirth of a collective NHS and, although many new chairs and non-executive directors have been appointed to trust boards in the period since the election, the executives remain the same individuals who were confronting their partners in the last contracting round of the internal market.

Local authorities are also seen as key partners in delivering the new health agenda and in ensuring public accountability through their involvement in local health decision making. There is no line management between central and local government and no pre-existing duty on local authorities to take any interest in health matters. The strategy requires that this be changed and a statutory duty is being placed on local authorities to support the health agenda in the 1999 Health Act. Through the National Priorities Guidance, combining the priorities and responsibilities of the NHS and social services, it is also clear that health authorities will be held to account both for the performance of local authorities in their support role and to provide support to local authorities in meeting their own responsibilities.

Direction, vision or detail?

The production of a comprehensive policy document such as this White Paper naturally poses as many questions as it answers. The absence of detail in many of the proposals helped to avoid opposition in the early stages. As far as the principles go, there was unlikely to be systematic opposition as the proposals did offer a relatively painless way out of the stifling bureaucracy and increasing pointlessness of the NHS internal market. While ministers spoke about allowing local solutions to emerge, that is not the style of the civil service. At least 62 working groups were set up by the DoH to provide guidance on the issues raised in the White Paper; the fact that such guidance was not really sought by NHS managers does not affect this behaviour. There was so much energy in NHS management to take forward the agenda described in the following pages, that the guidance was never likely to be in time; a case of guidance expected rather than guidance awaited. In the event, the DoH excelled itself in its tardiness in producing the small amount of guidance that was required and reached new heights in unfulfilled promises in terms of the timing of guidance. For example, the spring (1998) guidance on the development of HImPs became the July guidance, then the autumn guidance and finally reached the NHS long after most health authorities had written their first drafts.

In this book, I will describe the main changes proposed in the White Paper, supplemented by further detailed documentation and consultation papers released during 1998 and 1999; the impact these changes will have on the working lives of health service staff, the underlying themes in policy which are driving the changes and the potential fulfilment of these policies for health and healthcare.

Part 2

The facts, the proposals, the reasons

The Foreword

Tony Blair's initial message sets the scene, placing *The New NHS* in the context of its own history and, especially, the Labour Party's role in its creation. Apart from self-praise for the achievements hitherto in this parliament (extra funding for the NHS, renewed PFI for hospitals and an investment focus on breast cancer and paediatric intensive care – rather cheekily described here as 'children's services'), Mr Blair introduces the new language of the NHS: replacing the internal market with integrated care, saving £1 billion of red tape, combining efficiency and quality with a belief in fairness and partnership – the language of the successful election campaign. The buzzword throughout is modernisation, characterised best by the desire to use electronic communications as effectively as in other industries, such as banking. The promise of extra funding comes with a trade off: a responsibility within the service to change, to provide better care when it is needed and care of a uniformly high standard.

Modernisation reflecting the expectations of our community

requires a concerted effort at all levels. Modern Britain does not expect to wait for service, does expect full disclosure of detailed and relevant information, and demands a style of service which puts the customer/user first. This is not yet the culture of the healthcare industry but we must assume that it will increasingly become so. The utterly negative image of older aspects of the NHS estate also need attention, although they have not been specifically addressed in this White Paper.

Chapter 1: A modern and dependable NHS: there when you need it

Speed and efficiency

This is not a summary, more of a scene setting. Speed is the key issue and the analysis of weaknesses and solutions focuses on rapidity of response as the panacea. The problems of the NHS are described in terms of delays in treatment, variable quality and too much administration. Tom Peters, the American management guru, regards speed in administration and customer services as the key to competitiveness in a market situation. Having attempted to extend the principles to public services, he came to the conclusion that the political angle, lack of belief and an unwillingness to invest in communications technology prevented the forces of the market from operating and therefore benefiting from investment in speed-focused technology. It is not clear in *The New NHS* where the forces and drivers are for speed in administration and customer service other than altruism; the market is clearly not one.

There is a formal rejection of the widely held view that taxes (or, alternatively, charges) must rise or rationing must be introduced. Much is made of the variations in practice and variable efficiency among service providers and it is concluded that greater efficiency will deliver most of the resources required to enhance quality. It is implied that all variations can be abolished and that all providers can attain the standards of the best. Variations, however, are of two types; systematic variation which is due to controllable behaviour, and random variation which is due to chance. The former can be addressed by management action, leading to changes in practice and improvements in efficiency, but random variation will always persist. The government shows no sign of understanding this distinction.

The health of the people

The public health context is emphasised from the outset with a commitment to improve health and reduce inequalities in health, and the role of the Green Paper *Our Healthier Nation* is trailed (it had already been drafted). The government gives itself ten years to renew and improve the NHS, a realistic time frame in terms of the challenges and possibly in terms of electoral politics, allowing themselves scope for limited success in their 'first' term in power. The basic principle of local doctors and nurses having the best understanding of patients' needs is promoted (in the context of PCGs) but is extended, without evidence, to the task given to them in shaping local (specialist) services. This extrapolation of the principle is rejected by many consultants who spent the eight years of the fundholding scheme defending their services against the very mixed views and very variable knowledge of primary care commissioners. Indeed, there is no reason why generalists should be in any position to judge the value of specialists. Perhaps it might be considered that they are better placed than anyone else and certainly more balanced in their views than the specialists themselves. There are consistent references to a growing role for community nurses; a cynic's view would be that this is partly to dilute the power of doctors, partly for populist reasons and least, perhaps, for their distinctive contribution.

Realising the benefits of technology

The government commits itself to achieving a goal which has eluded all its predecessors, namely the harnessing of information (communications) technology to the benefit of operational health services and to improve the experiences of patients. Three symbolic examples of the location of these benefits are given in the White Paper to demonstrate the characteristics of a modernised NHS: at home, in the community and in hospital. Key elements of the new service include a 24-hour telephone advice line (NHS Direct) staffed by nurses and giving health and healthcare advice to help people care for themselves at home (three pilot projects, in Milton Keynes, Newcastle and Northumberland, and around Preston, were operating by March 1998, with progressive roll-out to achieve universal coverage by the end of 2000); by connecting all GP surgeries to the NHSnet (an industry-wide intranet with appropriate security for confidential patient information) the results of investigations will be available faster and outpatient appointments can be booked direct (demonstration sites chosen and established in each region at the end of 1998, test results accessible in all computerised practices by the end of 1999 (semi-abandoned after representations by the profession) and in all practices by 2002); the symbol for hospitals is to guarantee patient access to specialist assessment within two weeks for anyone with suspected cancer (for breast cancer by 1999 and for all other cancers one year later).

Greater detail on all these proposals, the benefits patients can expect and how the modernisation fund will be used to fund the strategy were published in a strategy for NHS information and information and communication technology (*Information for Health*) in summer 1998.

There will be those in the NHS who regard these targets as unachievable and others who consider them of subsidiary importance in the context of the problems facing the NHS. For example, no need had been demonstrated for an open-access telephone advice line and no quantification of the impact existed. Banking has demonstrated the value of such a service to their business, but the NHS is a different sort of business. However, the real disappointment is that these proposals are startlingly unambitious for a truly modern health service. In most leading edge health and healthcare systems for example, a two-day, rather than two-week, wait for investigation of possible cancer would be the maximum acceptable, yet there will be managers and clinicians who suggest that giving a two-week commitment for cancer patients will distort other health-care priorities.

Early experience with the NHS Direct pilots showed that the use of telephone advice lines was a surprisingly effective means of enabling access to health professionals by the public. The government has it in mind to extend the brief of NHS Direct to all first contacts with NHS services, including calls to GPs. Creating a single portal of entry to all NHS advice and patient services will, it is believed, save time and money and improve the internal communication of information. It is also claimed that the initial use of NHS Direct pilots to field calls to GPs led to a diversion to other (non-NHS) services of the order of 20%; the government is hopeful that the extended use of NHS Direct in this way may help to halt, or at least slow, the steep rise in demand for NHS services. In an unplanned development of the original idea, NHS Direct is now hoped to be a major driver of change, not in duplicating or substituting GPs' work but in changing the nature of their work.

Waiting times again

In addition to these specific benefits, the government repeated its commitment to reduce waiting lists by 100 000 (approximately 9%) during the life of this parliament, a relaxation from the manifesto which promised this reduction within a year. This change was in recognition of the short-term pressures facing the NHS during 1997/98. After this initial relaxation of its aspirations for waiting lists, the government pushed forward with targets for the reduction in numbers waiting as well as waiting times by the year 2002, that is the end of its five-year term. The government had already been warned that, without extra resources, a 10% increase in efficiency would be required each year to achieve its election commitment to reduce the number waiting by 100 000. The government's response was to invest an additional £500 million in 1998/99 to help reduce waiting lists in anticipation of the benefits for the NHS of the Comprehensive Spending Review. This investment proved immediately successful in halting the rise in waiting lists, albeit aided by vigorous validation of waiting lists and some reclassification of cases, and by the end of 1998 waiting lists were almost back to their March 1997 level. An influenza outbreak in December 1998, and a partial breakdown of primary care cover over the

Christmas period, led to a brief increase in waiting lists before normal service was resumed. Unfortunately, by investing more in surgical capacity to reduce waiting lists, the government has merely commenced the next supply and demand cycle which will lead to supply-led demand and an eventual increase in waiting lists again unless even more resources are committed to reducing them progressively.

The waiting list initiative, and the diversion of resources from other priorities – especially those of their own choosing – to feed it, has led to a good deal of anger in the medical fraternity. Most doctors do not regard waiting lists and times with the same importance as politicians do, but it is the latter who best reflect the mood of the public. People should not have to wait for treatment which is deemed to be necessary. Paying patients do not wait and any government which is truly committed to the success of the NHS will want to reduce the differences between the public and private healthcare.

The simmering conflict between politicians and the professions over the priority which should be afforded to reducing waiting lists reflects a wider agenda about who knows best in healthcare. Doctors have long believed that only they can and should decide what needs to be done to improve services and it is the responsibility of the government to pay for whatever they want to do. The government decides political priorities and expects its paid servants, including NHS doctors, to deliver for it.

The funding is sufficient if we use it well

The chapter continues with an interesting analysis of the big picture for tax-funded healthcare. It rejects the notion that the challenges of balancing need, demand and affordability are too great to meet head on and promotes a rationalist view of a safe and successful future for the NHS. Specifically, it acknowledges that the demand side is rising through public expectation, medical technological advances and demography (the ageing population). It makes the fascinating, and probably true, observations that the pressures on the NHS have always been exaggerated – a point hammered home after the excellent financial settlement for the NHS in 1999 accompanied by apparently crippling inflationary pressures, the fact that 70% of the demographic pressures to confront the NHS in the 20 years from 1988 have already been accommodated (regarded as 80% by the Royal Commission on Long Term Care published in March 1999) and, more controversially, that technology and public health action will take the pressure off healthcare. This last point is almost certainly misguided.

The case for technology is based on several misconceptions. These include the idea that less invasive interventions are necessarily cheaper, that angioplasty (incorrectly described as heart catheters) will replace coronary artery bypass grafts, that day surgery replaces expensive inpatient care (partly true) and that successful public health action reduces the burden on healthcare services. In practice, while there is some truth in all but the last of these, the general trend is for new technologies to add to the scope and range of care options and not to substitute for existing ones. This is particularly so for minimally invasive surgery, angioplasty and day surgery, all of whose development has fuelled large increases in activity and overall increases in costs. The assumption that better public health will reduce the burden on the NHS is, I believe, completely wrong. Effective public health postpones disease and death until old age, when the burden of disease falls greater on health services due to the combined dependency of disease and the frailty of old age. A long-lived population experiences fewer early deaths but higher levels of chronic disability; this is the factor which converts ageing into care costs.

The additional funding made available to the NHS through the Comprehensive Spending Review raised hopes and expectations, among staff and public, about the financial prospects for the service and the pace with which it could develop. It soon became clear early in 1999 that inflation created by government action was poised to use most of the new money, mainly on pay for doctors and nurses, higher costs for blood and blood products, capital charges inflation, changes to national insurance, the implementation of the so-called Social Chapter of the 1991 Maastricht Treaty – vigorously opposed by the previous government – and big increases in transport costs through successive budgets.

Keep the bureaucracy at bay

The case for rationing is rejected in favour of making better use of existing resources, especially through the diversion of management costs into frontline services. The magical figure of £1 billion is declared as a reduction in management costs over the lifetime of the current parliament. This was delivered in stages with a major contribution from an early start – £500 million from the £100 million reduction declared in 1997/98 (times five) and £320 million from the £80 million announced for 1998/99 (times four). By the end of the parliament, with the remaining £180 million being released from 1999/2000 onwards through mergers, further reductions in GP commissioning costs and reductions in NHS Executive headquarters costs, the annual saving on management costs compared with 1996/97 (the last full year of the last government) will be £240 million, less than 0.7% of NHS costs in England.

There is also a firm lead on harnessing new developments rather than merely reacting to commercially produced technologies. The systematic approach developed by the research and development strategy to testing and evaluating new technologies has to be translated into a systematic approach to basing clinical and managerial decisions on reliable evidence. The use of systematic cost-effectiveness evidence is also promoted, a signal that the rationing debate is not yet dead and characterised by the government's willingness to consider restricting the availability of Viagra (sildenafil). If only systematic cost-effectiveness evidence were widely available to inform such decisions, more benefit could reasonably be expected.

Power with responsibility for clinicians

A key innovation is the alignment of clinical and financial responsibility, effectively among groups of GPs. Professionals who make prescribing and referring decisions must now make these decisions in the best interests of their patients, knowing that they have a single, integrated budget to cover the costs. The budget for PCGs will include the costs of primary care prescribing, commissioning agreed elements of secondary care and the cash-limited budget for developing practice facilities. This integration creates opportunities to improve the rationality of investment across sectors of care and also removes some of the perverse incentives created by the separation of the primary care and secondary care budgets in the past, especially in terms of prescribing responsibility split between general practice and hospitals.

The NHS is cheap

An unexpected claim is made in the penultimate paragraph, namely that the national economy depends on the NHS. This is a recognition of the fact that, in economic terms, expenditure on healthcare is essentially unproductive. This is not a repeat of the naiveté of the Beveridge proposals, which anticipated that more healthcare would create a healthier and more efficient and productive workforce; it is a recognition that the low costs and relatively high efficiency of the NHS compared with other national health systems relieves the nation's industry of a major tax and/or cost burden. Public expenditure on healthcare becomes taxation in due course; private expenditure on healthcare is a cost to the whole economy.

The government has set out to reconnect with health service staff. The desire is to motivate staff to perform at exceptional levels of efficiency, quality and customer service. A relatively generous pay settlement for staff in 1999 led the way for unrealistic expectations during 1999/2000 and beyond. The use of the modernisation fund to pay for part of the pay award signals the government's intention to demand radical change in exchange for additional investment. Surprisingly, the failure of the government to fully fund the pay award attracted almost no publicity and no adverse news for the government. However, the inevitable consequence of high pay awards, high expectations of service growth and few really free resources for locally determined developments means that staff and the public will become increasingly disappointed and that, eventually, even jobs will be lost. The government will be keen to avoid the crisis that such an analysis would lead to, so either more funding will be made available or pay will be restrained again or both.

Chapter 2: A new start: what counts is what works

The third way

The government rejects a return to the pre-reform structure, as much, perhaps, for the precedent it would set for other sectors as for its impact on the NHS. It also, of course, rejects the status quo and describes its proposals as 'the third way', implying a difference rather than a combination. The 'third way' terminology is appearing with increasing frequency in cabinet statements, but appears to be the Prime Minister's personal message; it appears to seek a middle way between the social exclusion which results from unfettered capitalism and the stifling of energy which accompanies statism. It is an attempt to emulate the American Democratic Party, a one nation, socially conscious party which still upholds, with passion, the American dream. Mr Blair's party learned from President Clinton's electoral pragmatism, recognising that it is the middle classes that win elections. In the NHS context, this is the difference between the 'divisive internal market system' (of the Tories) and the 'command and control systems' of the 70s (under both parties). Unfairness and bureaucracy are seen as the enemies and collaboration as the basic element of success. Six key principles are described (Box 2.1) which underlie the changes proposed. These principles appear later under various guises, including the performance framework.

Among the 'not broken so won't be fixed' elements of the service it inherited, the government will retain the separation between the planning of hospital care and its provision, the central role of primary care and the devolved responsibilities of trusts. The so-called purchaser/provider split is now confined to secondary care and is relabelled 'planning'. GPs are retained in pole position, against the core political philosophy, because it is impossible to control anything if they are outside the structure. The government has been shrewd in amending its traditional stance on GPs, and retaining them as key players, but I am less sure that they have judged the uncertain mood among GPs as keenly as they might. In particular, there is a need for visible and positive incentives for GPs

---

Box 2.1   Six key principles for *The New NHS*

- A genuinely national service; fair access to consistently high-quality, prompt and accessible services

- The delivery of healthcare against new national standards to be a matter of local responsibility

- The needs of the patient will be put at the centre of the care process; the NHS will work in partnership with local authorities

- Drive efficiency through a more rigorous approach to performance and by cutting bureaucracy

- Shift the focus on to quality of care so that excellence is guaranteed and quality becomes the driving force

- Rebuild public confidence in the NHS, accountable to patients, open to the public and shaped by their views

---

to retain the enthusiasm they showed for fundholding in the face of vigorous opposition in 1991. To date, the incentives remain largely altruistic rather than tangible, and certainly less attractive than under the fundholding scheme. Retaining a range of trust freedoms for operational services merely recognises the turmoil that any other strategy would entail and continues to locate some of the more serious service failures at some distance from government itself. It is often useful for politicians to have someone else to blame! In contrast, the proposals purport to end the fragmentation, unfairness, distortion, inefficiency, bureaucracy, instability and secrecy of the internal market. The first move was to require trusts to hold their meetings in public.

Fragmentation

Here we are introduced to the idea that there are 4000 organisations in the NHS, comprising 100 health authorities, 400 trusts and 3500 GP fundholders. Much is made later of the reduction in the number of NHS organisations, but most observers would question whether fundholding practices rate as organisations alongside either existing health authorities and trusts or the prospective PCGs. Notwithstanding the play on numbers, the introduction of a local joint planning process, leading to the production of a jointly agreed HImP is a clear signal to all agencies that collectivism is back and, with the added involvement of social care, with a vengeance.

Unfairness

It is implied that competition and unfairness are inevitable companions and that the competitive values upset the sensitivities of professional staff. While this is undoubtedly true up to a point, it has been the natural competitiveness of staff that has both enabled and driven the internal market reforms of the previous government. Admittedly, some of this competitiveness, both of organisations and of individuals, was conceived in an atmosphere of survival of the fittest and the competitive behaviour which followed was clearly defensive in intent. However, repairing the splits in professions created by optional structures, especially fundholding, has been generally welcomed, suggesting a discomfort in some members of the professions with open competitiveness. Needs-based treatment and professional cooperation are the new rules and influence is guaranteed for community nurses, often the least consulted constituency, and specialist clinicians, previously over-consulted prior to the internal market which transferred so much power to management.

Distortion

The effect of markets is to distort a steady state leading to a reshaping of the service provider community. The NHS internal market did not lead to the indicated reshaping of provision of healthcare because the politicians of the day were not prepared to see through the consequences of operating a market. Here it is the quasi-commercial ownership of information and intellectual property by NHS trusts that comes under the cosh from the government. The answer, they say, will be the systematic sharing of best practice, and variable performance standards will be addressed by a new national performance framework covering the six key principles. The perceived pressures and unrealised forces of the market will be replaced by public contestability of the performance of providers by publishing the results of patient treatment and efficiency.

Inefficiency

This is an immensely popular and justified assault on the Purchaser Efficiency Index, arguably the most absurd performance monitoring vehicle yet invented in the UK. It measured change in the purchasing of healthcare at the margin and took it to describe performance at the core. It encouraged perverse (unnecessary) surgical activity and constituted a disincentive to effective care. For example, the desired reduction in unnecessary diagnostic Ds & Cs was complicated by the fact that they are usually performed as day cases, which have been regarded as a universal good thing. Indeed, all activity was regarded as good, however pointless it may have been clinically. The obsession with measured hospital activity persists, however, fuelled by the matching political imperative of waiting list reduction. Even by the year 2000, the only measure of activity and efficiency for which the NHS will be held to account is the cost and count of acute hospital admissions.

The separation of different parts of the NHS budget, long seen as a protection for patients, also comes in for criticism. The integration of budgets is a central element of the financial changes but may prove to be an Achilles heel if, for example, prescribing costs rise steeply – as has happened before – and then impact on the funding of hospital services. Indeed, one of the first unwelcome surprises for health authorities that were implementing the integrated budget was the need to provide for prescribing inflation – variously estimated at 7 to 11.5% – out of the 2.5% allocated to overall NHS budgets for inflation in 1999/2000.

We are promised better measures of real efficiency; the absence of detail or even ideas, and the lack of response to consultation on the issue – other than to criticise the efficiency index and the need to include activity in outpatients and the community that prevents hospitalisation – exposes the challenge in fulfilling this promise. Various government initiatives to promote the development of services that embrace several sectors of healthcare and social care (whole systems) have created innovative service models which avoid hospitalisation. Under the tools of measurement now in use, these models of care have no value yet they reflect the principles and values of the government.

Bureaucracy

The implementation of the previous government's reforms increased management costs by 1% of total NHS revenue. Recent cuts in management costs at all levels have already released more than this since 1993, but some of these reductions are masked by redefinitions. With such a busy management agenda, and with universal organisational change, further steep reductions in management seriously threaten the ability of the NHS to manage at all. The reduction of £1 billion during the lifetime of the parliament is, as already indicated, a neat trick with numbers; statistically correct but of limited impact. As a manager, I would have to say that it could have been worse.

The new NHS has an inbuilt tension between the size of the new organisations and the cost of running them. Many Labour politicians have an intrinsic resistance to large, remote structures, based on their previous experience of Conservative-led county councils. In consequence, PCGs were sized at a relatively small 100 000 population; small that is for efficiency in funding their boards, but arguably too large for effective commissioning of basic services (according to the evaluation of the first two generations of total purchasing projects). The opportunity to massively reduce management costs in this area of the service, following the abolition of GP fundholding in 1999, was therefore lost. An entirely different approach was taken in Scotland, where large GP-led commissioning groups (the equivalent of primary care trusts south of the border) were established from the outset.

Instability

This is really about replacing contracts with agreements and substituting long-term arrangements for annual and cost-per-case contracts. In most places, the change will be modest because major shifts in services have been rare and most contracts are simply cost and activity rationalisations. It is the culture that will change rather than the currency. The inclusiveness of the HImP (medium-term plans, drafted and agreed by all local agencies) and the unification of commissioning at PCG and health authority level reduce the scale and frequency of change. There is little in the White Paper about the role of the private sector, but up to £100 million annually of fundholder expenditure on private providers of elective surgery and community-based therapies could be restored to the NHS family over time. The government's continued antagonism to private healthcare, contrasting with its love affair with private investment in public partnership initiatives, is a hangover of old Labour thinking, but it also reflects the perverse position of the chief beneficiaries of private healthcare, i.e. doctors employed more or less full time by the NHS.

Secrecy

An interesting departure into the original language of *Working for Patients*, which also used the term 'self-governing' to describe NHS trusts, introduces this conversion from commercialism to collectivism. Trust boards are now required to meet in public, a new challenge for many members, but one tackled with surprisingly little hard work for PR rescue merchants. We are also introduced to the publication of trust performance data, the real means of accountability, and the consequent naming and shaming which will inevitably result. Two other nuances are apparent: the greater openness at local level seeks to compensate for the continuation of central control of the NHS and the democratic deficit which so motivated Labour while in opposition; and a promise of additional funding each year but on condition that it delivers major gains in quality and efficiency (subsequently agreed at 3% per annum) – no change in policy there then.

The effectiveness of our democracy relies on a balance of power between the main parties. A lack of effective opposition is a serious obstacle to democracy. The ineffectiveness of the Conservative opposition after the 1997 general election protected the government from the noise it ought to have expected in creating NHS inflation and from the blind eye it turned to the fixes (validation and reclassification) which enabled waiting lists to fall for political advantage; only the indomitable Ann Widdecombe spoke out effectively against the government. More recently, a junior opposition health spokesman, Alan Duncan, has restated the Conservative belief that a growing private sector helps the NHS; evidence to support this policy is awaited with interest. A speech by the deputy leader of the Conservative Party, Peter Lilley, attempted to distance the Party from a commitment to further privatisation, especially in health and education. The fierce opposition this line encountered within Tory ranks exposes the continuing confusion of opposition policy on health, and led to the premature retirement of Mr Lilley from high office.

Chapter 3: Driving change in the NHS: quality and efficiency hand in hand

Restructure and change the paradigm

The new NHS structures and their roles are introduced together with the features of the new performance and quality standards. Quality is described in broad terms; doing the right things, at the right time, for the right people and doing them right first time – alternatively interpreted as effective, timely, appropriate and efficient. The process is important as well as the outcome.

Once again the internal market is portrayed as the criminal, distracting NHS staff from their main purpose of caring. There is concern at the serious lapses of quality which have harmed patients and dented public confidence. This is a reference to several highly publicised failures of screening programmes for breast and cervical cancer and to errors in pathology and radiotherapy services. The experience of these, and the absence of any action against the professional culprits, is what lies behind the new statutory responsibility for quality and the accountability of trust chief executives. There is no mention of the powers that chief executives can exercise internally to deal with failing professionals; this is presumably too sensitive at this stage, but a necessary addition. If poor performance is to be eliminated, it must be made easier to dismiss incompetent doctors.

A First Class Service was published in June 1998 to expand upon the basic ideas and structures described in this chapter of the White Paper. Its timing was fortuitous, coming shortly after the celebrated public hearing at the GMC where a group of 'distinguished' doctors and their manager (also a doctor) were struck off the register (or in one case suspended) as a result of their failure to follow the principles now outlined in the government's proposals. Such was the public mood of disgust with the behaviour of the professions, not just the individuals concerned nor indeed necessarily cognisant of the facts, that the agencies representing the medical profession (the GMC itself, the British Medical Association (BMA) and the medical Royal Colleges and Faculties) felt obliged to support the government's caustic initiative against the independence and continuing self-determination of the profession. As a result, all health professions are on trial and, with the new powers acquired by the government to vary the terms of professional self-regulation through the 1999 Act, the screw is bound to tighten on the professions throughout the life of this parliament.

Quality

The example of the Calman–Hine report on the commissioning of cancer services, a unique exercise in central planning during the era of the market-obsessed previous government, is used to promote the advantages of the new programme of evidence-based NSFs. As with the prototype cancer strategy, the goal of the service frameworks will be consistency of access to uniformly high quality care.

A National Institute for Clinical Excellence (NICE) will provide the long-awaited link between the NHS research and development strategy and the operational NHS. The Institute will draw up or commission evidence-based guidelines for clinical services and disseminate them throughout the NHS; neither function has been systematically and comprehensively performed hitherto.

At local level, the responsibility for raising the quality of services will fall to GPs and community nurses working together in PCGs, service agreements between all NHS bodies encompassing national standards and a new system of clinical governance in all providers, which is defined in *A First Class Service* (see Part 4). Of these, it is the clinical governance initiative – guidance on which was published at Easter 1999 – that holds the key, together with the reserve powers retained by the government to intervene. Such intervention will be triggered by reports from a new Commission for Health Improvement (CHI), which will act as an inspectorial body for poorly performing providers.

The 1999 White Paper on public health (*Saving Lives: Our Healthier Nation*) introduces a body similar to NICE for public health and health promotion, the Health Development Agency.

Efficiency

Variations in efficiency are as unfair to patients as are variations in quality, as inefficiency deprives patients of access to services. Five approaches are adopted to secure improvements in efficiency (Box 2.2). The integration of budgets and the alignment of clinical and financial responsibility are acts of faith. I am not aware of any reason to assume that they will lead to greater efficiency; it is more likely that they will increase the risk to PCG solvency. The reductions in management costs have largely been achieved already and the service is at risk of becoming under-managed. The real crunch for providers is the proposed publication of reference costs and their imposition as standards to beat by trusts whose performance will be calculated and therefore published by the government; another example of naming and shaming. This is how the government intends for costs to be reduced and resources released from hospital services in particular. The incentives and sanctions are less important for their ultimate value and more so for the impact they have on the willingness of GPs to engage actively in PCGs an engagement which was in the balance at one stage. Eventually, most PCGs actually managed to recruit enough GPs to fill their board places, though rarely with a lot of enthusiasm. It has been more a case of not wishing to be outflanked than to seize the opportunity. Involvement in management does tend to be seductive, however, and the commitment to improve and change services will come in due course.

Box 2.2   Ensuring efficiency in *The New NHS*

- Aligning clinical and financial responsibility and devolving responsibility for a single unified budget to PCGs; this will cover most services and will offer incentives at PCG and practice level

- Management costs will be capped in health authorities and PCGs and reduced in trusts

- The government will publish reference costs for individual treatments and will require trusts to make known, and to benchmark, their own costs

- There will be cash incentives to improve performance and efficiency for health authorities, trusts and PCGs

- Sanctions can be imposed on poor performers, including withdrawal of freedoms (from PCGs), and the right to move services between providers is retained. Direct intervention by the NHS Executive is also possible.

Measurement

The new performance framework – encompassing the measurement of health improvement, fairer access to services, quality and outcomes, the views of patients and real efficiency – is introduced briefly on the principle of 'what gets measured gets done'. In the past, the wrong things were measured and management was perverse, that is, it addressed the measured elements rather than the important things; the wrong measures produced the wrong results; the unavoidable squeezed out the necessary. This is fair comment, but it is not easy to monitor performance against things we have never measured and data we do not collect. The government appears willing to invest in information technology to overcome this problem and is determined to successfully apply technological solutions to the age-old challenge of health data that are timely, relevant and of high quality. However, the examples given in the White Paper and repeated as exemplars in 'Information for Health' (Box 2.3) have the appearance of a textbook rather than a realisable strategy.

Box 2.3 Information technology for quality and efficiency

- Making patients' records electronically available

- Using the NHSnet and the Internet to deliver test results quickly, on-line booking of appointments and up-to-date advice

- Prompt financial and performance information

- Using the Internet and digital TV to provide knowledge on health, illness and treatment for the public

- Introducing telemedicine to disseminate specialist skills to all parts of the country

---

Roles and responsibilities

The roles of the main structures of the new NHS are outlined, with more detailed analysis in subsequent chapters. The health authorities will be the planning agencies, PCGs are the focus of integrated care, NHS trusts will be specialist providers and the DoH will integrate health and social care policy and will try to control the professions.

Chapter 4: Health authorities: leading and shaping

In charge

Health authorities will be the strategic leaders of the local NHS and their stronger role will overcome the fragmentation of previous structures and especially the internal market. This is a criticism of the freedoms given to both trusts and fundholders in the previous reforms. Health authority functions are summarised in Box 2.4.

Many of these functions are new to health authorities and others are greatly enhanced. With little preparation and no tangible support, and the inevitable continuing squeeze on management costs, health authorities managed to establish PCGs and to initiate the new planning processes and even drew praise from ministers – though only in private. Later, a full year after publication of the White Paper, a special initiative was launched at the NHS Executive to explore and implement the development of the role of health authorities.

Box 2.4   The functions of the new health authorities

- Assessing the health needs of the local population

- Drawing up a HImP to meet those needs, in partnership with local interests

- Deciding the range and location of healthcare services for the authority's residents

- Setting local targets and standards to drive quality and efficiency and ensuring their delivery

- Supporting the development of PCGs

- Allocating resources to PCGs

- Holding PCGs to account

Health first

Public health policy is the lead-off point, enshrined in a new proposed statutory duty to improve the health of populations. Health authorities will work with local authorities and others to identify where local action is necessary. Specific areas of public health action will include communicable disease control, health needs assessment, monitoring health outcomes and evaluating the health impact of local plans and developments. There is nothing new in any of this, but health authorities have always had to do other things on which their performance was judged; public health performance has not been important hitherto until things go wrong. The Director of Public Health's annual report will be the starting point for the HImP. To achieve this, the reports and the public health function will both have to improve a lot. A separate investigation, by the former Chief Medical Officer Sir Kenneth Calman, into the public health function produced an irritatingly incomplete and complicated interim report which told the service nothing it did not already know; the final report was delayed for a year while the public health White Paper was being drafted.

The HImP will be the local health and healthcare strategy. It will detail how the new national targets are to be met. Health authorities will lead the other NHS (NHS trusts and PCGs) and local authority-related (social services, education, housing, police, probation, fire) organisations and the independent contractor professions in developing the HImP. Local authorities and NHS bodies will have a statutory responsibility of partnership, incorporated into the 1999 Health Act. The HImP will cover the health needs of the population, the healthcare requirements to meet those needs and the range, location and investment in health services required. The HImP will be a three-year rolling plan with annual updates. As they are responsible for the delivery of the NHS components of the plan, health authorities will have important new reserve powers over NHS trust spending decisions, including capital plans and new consultant posts. The health authorities are also given responsibility for coordinating workforce education plans and, of more urgency, coordinating information and information technology plans across the whole of the NHS in their area (this includes the development of primary care computing, including links to the NHSnet, and managing the year 2000 date change problem with computer chips. Health authorities do not have the skills to do this; but then nor does anyone else in the NHS). The effectiveness of historical cooperation with local authorities is seen as a problem by the government; in future, under the aegis of the initiative on 'Better Services for Vulnerable People', health authorities and social services will have to produce three-year joint investment plans (JIPs) for these vulnerable groups, including children, mentally ill people, people with learning difficulties, disabled people and older people. These are to be completed by April 2000, with at least one completed by April 1999. Indeed, it is certainly possible that this framework could ultimately replace the existing social services responsibility for the production of children's services plans and JIPs will replace the annual community care plan. Pooled budgets and other stimuli to close working are envisaged. A further Green Paper, *Partnership in Action*, published in the summer of 1998, proposed various new mechanisms for joint working at strategic, commissioning and operational levels and foresaw the redundancy of the statutory Joint Consultative Committees, once better local arrangements have been established.

There is an interesting aside to the use of acronyms for the Health Improvement Programme. Originally shortened to HIP, local authorities pointed out that they already had a HIP (Housing Investment Plan) so the awkward acronym HImP was coined as a compromise.

Devolving commissioning but staying in control

Health authorities will devolve responsibility for commissioning of services to PCGs as soon as possible. This harnesses the strategic view of health authorities and the innovative energies of primary care. However, health authorities will probably still be responsible for commissioning highly specialised tertiary services, under collaborative arrangements to be determined by NHS Executive Regional Offices. A separate consultation conducted during the summer of 1998 into the scope and arrangements for specialist commissioning led to an extended list of services and new regional structures for overseeing this work.

The national targets set out in *Our Healthier Nation* will form the basis of HImPs to improve health, and PCGs will have to commission services accordingly. PCGs and NHS trusts will be held to account for delivering their elements of the HImP and any disputes will be resolved by health authorities; this gives them a responsibility previously held only by regional health authorities prior to their abolition in 1996.

Accountable to the people

In addition to these management functions, health authorities will be expected to involve local people more effectively to build a new public confidence in the NHS. Using the simple maxim of the NHS being responsive and accountable, health authorities will involve the public in developing the HImP, ensure that PCGs involve the public in the conduct of their work, publish their strategies and progress, and participate in the new user and patient survey. It is, in my view, unlikely that any of these actions will increase public confidence; that will only come from more tangible investment in the NHS, rising standards of service, less naming and blaming, and fewer complaints of cuts and crises from staff.

The government will enable these actions to be realised (Box 2.5) and this may lead to fundamental changes in the existing framework of NHS organisations. For example, aligning trust and PCG accountabilities with the HImP may ultimately lead to changes in health authority boundaries. This will distort coterminosity between NHS and local authorities, though this may matter less if social care responsibilities are increasingly integrated at PCG level. The provision for local authority chief executives to participate in health authority meetings has aroused mixed feelings, especially among elected members of local authorities. The government does not have the same management relationship with local authorities as it has with the NHS, nor does it seem to be particularly interested in the maintenance of long-standing local democratic structures – preferring to prepare for the devolution of the government of services to regional assemblies in its second

> ### Box 2.5   Making it happen
>
> - Health authorities will have statutory responsibilities for improving the health of the population, and for working in partnership with other organisations
>
> - NHS trusts and PCGs will be responsible for working within the HImP; their responsibilities will be aligned within the health authority role
>
> - Local authority chief executives will participate in meetings of health authorities; the experience of HAZs will guide further strengthening of health and local authority partnership arrangements
>
> - Health authority administrative functions will be shared and streamlined, to release time, effort and resources (for the new role); fewer authorities covering larger areas will emerge as a result

term. Also, the role of chief executives in local authorities is less pre-eminent than in health authorities, while the role of the Council Leader is infinitely more so than that of NHS trust and health authority chairs.

This proposal could not be acted upon until the passing of the 1999 Act. The instinctive opposition of elected members to officer leadership has been somewhat mollified by the similar pressures being placed on local authorities in the management of their own business through the *Modernising Local Government* White Paper. From the government's point of view, the advantages of working through officers are the avoidance of petty politics, of accusations of bias and contamination with growing local sleaze. Furthermore, with the structure of local government in England resembling an unholy shambles (metropolitan districts, London boroughs, unitary authorities, Shire counties, district councils), a further revision of local government structures is inevitable, probably towards universal unitary authorities and equally probably associated with devolution to the regions in England.

The publication, for the first time ever, of joint National Priorities Guidance for health and social services, in the autumn of

1998, constituted a major symbolic and structural focus for joint planning and working between health authorities and social services departments. By requiring joint plans to be published, the accountabilities of the NHS and of local government become added together.

Subsequent negotiations suggested a tactical withdrawal from health authority mergers. A number of provincial urban conurbations were openly discussing major health authority mergers as early as the spring of 1998. A formal proposal from four health authorities in Greater Manchester to merge was rejected without ceremony when it was opposed by the local MPs. Similar proposals for West Yorkshire, Tyne and Wear, West Midlands, etc., were duly stillborn. The replacement as Health Minister of Alan Milburn by John Denham reduced further the probability of health authority mergers for the foreseeable future. However, I believe that the establishment of Tier 4 primary care trusts will lead to health authority mergers on a large scale by 2005.

Radical centralisation for GP administration

Of more profound significance to health authorities in the medium term might have been the so-called streamlining of their administrative functions. This is a euphemism for the centralisation of the administration of independent contractors, a role which currently occupies about one quarter of health authority headquarters staff. Ultimately, within ten years, there could be a single national agency for contractor support administration; in the interim, regional or subregional agencies were expected to be established within two or three years, with rationalisation into one or two agencies per region. In practice, little action has been taken in pursuit of these ideas, other than some local mergers of support functions already being planned or in place. Further moves in this direction are unlikely to be necessary to deliver the efficiency savings required to reach management cost targets and there appears to be startlingly little enthusiasm for radical restructuring of these services at the moment among ministers, GPs themselves or health authorities.

Chapter 5: Primary care groups: going with the grain

Still a primary care-led NHS?

The government does a fair job of declaring its support for broadly based primary care services. Later documents refer to 'keeping primary care in the driving seat', an example of the government's belief in the value of entrepreneurialism in public services. Their description of primary care covers the full range of professions and the great scope for the development of their role in the future. While recognising the importance of general practice, it is clear that the development of primary and community care lies largely in other areas of the service. While the independent contractor status of GPs is not directly affected by the proposals, over time, alternatives to independence will grow in number and attractiveness.

Learning from experience; PCGs

The government's proposals are allegedly based on the success of recent collective approaches to primary care-led commissioning, such as total purchasing pilots and multifunds, despite the absence of any completed evaluation of them at the time of publication of the White Paper and subsequent evidence that the proposed groupings are too large for effective and successful commissioning. The merits of empowering primary care are accepted without reservation as is the rejection of a competitive market. PCGs will be the manifestation of the new arrangements; unlike existing schemes of practice-based and local commissioning, they will be mandatory and universal from the outset, with a uniform structure and progressive increases in their responsibilities. Their functions, structure and requirements are summarised in Boxes 2.6–2.8.

Later guidance issued by the Health Minister, John Denham, redefines Level 3 organisations as trusts also. This clearly indicates the government's intention to move speedily to primary care trust coverage while retaining a degree of voluntary membership of the club. The expected surge of enthusiasm for early primary care trust

Box 2.6 The main functions of PCGs

- Contribute to the health authority's HImP on health and health-care, reflecting the perspective of the local community and the experience of patients

- Promote the health of the local population, in partnership with other agencies

- Commission health services from relevant NHS trusts, within the framework of the HImP

- Monitor performance against the service agreements they have with NHS trusts

- Develop primary care by joint working across practices; sharing skills; providing a forum for professional development, audit and peer review; developing the new approach to clinical governance

- Integrate primary and community health services and work more closely with social services on planning and delivery

Box 2.7 Options for the scope and responsibilities of PCGs

- **Level 1** Advise and support the health authority in commissioning care for its population

- **Level 2** Take devolved responsibility for managing the budget for healthcare in their area, formally as part of the health authority

- **Level 3** Become established as freestanding bodies accountable to the health authority for commissioning care

- **Level 4** As Level 3 but with added responsibility for the provision of community health services for their population

> ### Box 2.8   Common core requirements for PCGs
>
> - Representative of all the general practices in the group
> - A governing body which includes community nursing and social services as well as GPs drawn from the area
> - Take account of social services boundaries as well as health authority areas to help promote integration in service planning and provision
> - Abide by the local HImP
> - Clear arrangements for public involvement including open meetings
> - Efficient and effective arrangements for management and financial accountability

status has materialised (170 expressions of interest in the first wave, representing 36% of all PCGs, a far higher level of interest at this stage than shown for NHS trusts in 1990) and the probability exists that most of the country will be served by primary care trusts, at Levels 3 or 4, by 2002.

We can draw a number of inferences from the presentation of these characteristics. First, it is clear that PCGs are intended to be more like health authorities than any of the various forms of primary care commissioning previously operating. In particular, Level 4 primary care trusts will be vertically integrated organisations with responsibility for both the provision of care and the commissioning of health services. Second, the structural inclusion of community nursing and social care is both a logical boost to the integration of care and a systematic attempt to dilute the power and influence of doctors in these groups. Third, while there are four options for the development and scope of responsibilities of the groups, and groups will declare the position they wish to occupy on the scale at the outset (albeit subject to health authority approval), there is only one direction to travel (towards Level 4) and the overall strategy requires PCGs to progress quickly, with a significant minority at Level 3 by, say, 2001 at the latest. This is to enable health authorities to slim down and focus on their new role, relieved of the responsibility for commissioning services. Fourth, the potential creation of primary care trusts, the first of which could not be set up until April 2000 due to delays in securing the necessary legislation, has profound implications for existing NHS trusts. As Level 4 primary care trusts will manage community health services and community hospitals, these will have to be removed from existing trusts. Furthermore, a late decision by the NHS Executive to exclude mental health and learning disability services from PCGs, and the statement preferring specialist mental health trusts for these services, fundamentally changes NHS trust configuration in many places.

We face a service model, early in the life of the next parliament, where all primary and community services (including community hospitals) may be managed by primary care trusts, all mental health services and learning disability services will be in specialist NHS trusts or managed by primary care trusts under supervision of specialist providers, and the general and specialist hospital services will be all that remains for other NHS trusts. Radical reconfiguration of NHS trusts has been under way to establish these frameworks with general support from Labour MPs and from ministers. However, a discrete freeze has now been imposed on trust mergers until after the next general election, probably in 2001. There have been some reservations about the independence of primary care trusts and especially their role as employers of community staff. There are those who consider it safer for health authorities or NHS trusts to be the employers of convenience for these staff until primary care trusts have proved themselves, hence the creation of Level 3 primary care trusts. In practice, the untidiness of such a mixture is unlikely to be attractive and the emphasis instead will be on ensuring the success of the new trusts through tight line management.

A conundrum over mental health

There has been some discord in the DoH over the initial exclusion of mental health and learning disability services from higher level PCGs. The main concern of the proposers of these exclusions was the need to protect mental health services for political reasons, service failures being a particularly sensitive issue for ministers. However, the transfer of community services to PCGs will leave mental health services in limbo; their combination with acute general hospitals being regarded as unacceptable. Subsequent softening of the line suggests that once the new specialist trust arrangements are secure, community-based services for these groups may transfer to PCGs and trusts. Indeed, some are suggesting that almost all mental health services can be managed by primary care trusts, leaving only highly specialised and secure services for specialist providers. Such a service model is not sustainable unless primary care trusts cover larger populations than currently envisaged and specialist mental health providers are regional in scale.

The emerging framework for health and social services will require the reshaping of services in recognition of the key partnerships that are necessary to deliver the optimum success. A group of services will remain territorially based; these include primary care, community health services and social services. The structural focus for these services will be the primary care trust. Hospital services are no longer territorial but are based on the possession of skills. Their key partnerships are with highly specialised skills based in tertiary hospitals, although they do still require close operational links with community-based services. Mental health services comprise a mixture of territorial and skill-based services and do not fit this model comfortably. In short, mental health services will continue to be a problem and every structural solution will merely create its own set of problems.

Local and accountable

These primary care arrangements are accountable to health authorities, just as total purchasing pilots and multifunds were. The 481 newly established PCGs in England will cover populations of approximately 100 000, with the smallest being 42 000 and the largest over 250 000. The rules of configuration allow groups to cross health authority boundaries and individual practices can theoretically choose which group they belong to, and therefore which health authority they are part of. Groups are based on practices and do not have discrete geographical boundaries. Despite the extensive and confusing guidance, locally agreed proposals were likely to be accepted if they were supported by the local medical committee (LMC). Where the LMC objected, health authorities were leant on to give way but this could not be enforced despite the then minister, Alan Milburn, having apparently capitulated to all the profession's demands. Health and local authorities have fixed geographical boundaries which PCGs, being practice-based, inevitably breach. The establishment of primary care trusts on practice populations will create a major obstacle to partnership working at the boundaries. These characteristics may well lead to the subsequent redrawing of health authority boundaries but not, I suspect, in the short term.

The budgets available to these PCGs will be substantial (Box 2.9) and, for the first time, bring together all the costs of treating patients in the NHS. It is presumed that the integration of these budgets with financial and clinical responsibility will improve the quality of decision making. This may be true, but only the prescribing budgets will be practice-based initially. Later, indicative budgets will be extended for all aspects of NHS expenditure to practices, but this will be to sharpen accountability, not to delegate

---

Box 2.9   Unified PCG budgets

- The budget for the commissioning of all hospital and community health services

- The budget for the costs of drugs prescribed in primary care by doctors and nurses (there is an area of uncertainty here about the drugs prescribed by dentists)

- The cash-limited budget for general medical services infrastructure, used to reimburse practices for a proportion (usually 70%) of the cost of their practice staff and to meet part or all of the cost of practice premises and computers

- The average total budget for the average PCG will be of the order of £65 million at 1999/2000 value

control. All decisions by PCGs will be group-based; collectivism is back, individuality is relegated. However, groups may develop practice-based incentives in the future, although incentives are initially focused on prescribing and are closely related to the schemes used for non-fundholders up to 1999. There are basic flaws in these assumptions; if peer pressure is to be brought to bear on outlying practices (in terms of clinical behaviour and costs), then practice-level data will be required. However, the abandonment of practice-level data collection is a basic component of the abolition of fundholding and the move towards collective approaches to primary care-based commissioning. It is also necessary to stop collecting data in both commissioners and providers if the transaction costs of the internal market are to be slashed. At some point, the obsession with reducing management costs will abate and the need to secure control over expenditure will achieve precedence; perhaps practice-level data have not seen their armageddon just yet.

Managing the drug budget

The undoubted, if relative, success of the fundholding scheme in controlling the rise in expenditure on pharmaceuticals lies behind the integration of prescribing budgets with the commissioning funds for hospital and community health services. It also creates the Treasury's dream of at last being able to stop worrying about the rising drug bill; that pleasure now belongs to PCGs, as any rise in drug costs must be compensated for by a reduction in hospital costs. At approximately 12% of the total NHS cost, drugs are a major but not overwhelming component of NHS costs and pressures. In recent years, the proportion of total NHS spending used on pharmaceutical treatments has risen sharply and, as more expensive and effective drugs make their way on to the market, drugs will continue to increase as a share of total NHS expenditure. There is nothing wrong with this growth so long as the new drugs provide clinical value. Also, the fraught interface between hospital prescribing and community prescribing can now be relaxed. But the preferential prices at which drugs are sold to hospitals could now be under threat if, to save money, prescribing responsibility is transferred to hospitals. There is also clear evidence that dispensing general practices are disincentivised from delivering efficient prescribing, an issue which requires complex action (discussed later). The government has also found itself grappling with the tense relationship its predecessors enjoyed with the pharmaceutical industry, especially in terms of the NHS drug pricing regime. It has already indicated that the recovery of research and development costs through drug prices has such an impact on the total cost that the volume of R&D whose costs are recovered in this way might usefully be reviewed (downwards).

Tough times for fundholding staff

Because the whole PCG concept is based on collective approaches, little of the existing administration associated with practice-level involvement in fundholding has been required. The management costs of the scheme were therefore substantially reduced. Health authorities now have a management cost envelope which covers their own costs and those of the PCGs (covering functions which will become increasingly integrated). This cost envelope is set at a level below that which had been available previously to cover the health authority and fundholding management costs. However, the 10% cut in the fundholder management allowance for 1998/99 narrowed the gap and operating within the cost envelope should be feasible if duplication of data collection is avoided and PCGs are above the minimum size. However, NHS trusts must be able to demonstrate that they can deliver high-quality data which have the confidence of GPs; this was not generally the case with fundholders. The White Paper included a figure of £3 per head of population to support the running costs of PCGs. In fact, this was just an averaging of the surviving fundholder management allowance (after incremental cuts) shared equally across the country. PCGs also have a share of the health authority's commissioning resources to work with and, in Level 4 (commissioning and providing primary care trusts), a share of the management costs of community health services transferred from NHS trusts. For the probable minimum population of 100 000, a primary care trust may well have management cost allowances of well over £500 000.

The delay in securing the necessary legislation to abolish the fundholding scheme until after the beginning of 1999/2000 created a minor degree of chaos, with PCGs and fundholders both legally in existence. As the closure of fundholders' activities consumed some resources, PCGs were given a management cost allowance of only £2.47 per head of population for 1999/2000 and a total resource of £2.72 per head – the extra 25p to support their activities including those, such as clinical development, clinical governance and public health, which are excluded from management costs. It is assumed that the full £3.00 per head will be available to PCGs from 2000/01 onwards; for 1999/2000, the missing 28p has to be used by health authorities to manage the termination of the fundholding scheme. As many groups were slow to complete their key appointments, they managed to live within these constraints. However, a full-size PCG board, with a chief executive and an office, alone costs about £140 000 per annum, which is more than any group serving less than 60 000 people can afford.

Primary care trusts; into the (un)known

Further guidance has now been issued on the criteria and board structure for primary care trusts (see Part 5). It is clear, however, that they will remain accountable to health authorities, unlike NHS trusts, and will have to comply with corporate and clinical governance rules, including the appointment of the chief executive as the accountable officer. Such is the scale and scope of these responsibilities that they are likely to be fulfilled by professional managers and only exceptionally by GPs. This is the clearest signal that PCGs are not a development of fundholding but are a localisation of health authorities with the integration of primary and community care within a single accountable body, possibly with social care to follow.

The management implications

The level of management that has become commonplace in fundholding practices and in operational services in community care is characteristic of middle management, craving certainty and hoarding information. The type of management required for Level 3 (commissioning) primary care trusts and, especially, Level 4 (commissioning and providing) primary care trusts is very much higher. These more senior and capable managers thrive on paradox and uncertainty; their turnover in posts is higher, they take more risks and their approach is more appropriate to the excitement which trust status introduces. These management skills were only available in NHS trusts and health authorities, and just possibly some of the most advanced total purchasing pilots, and this is where the top managers of primary care trusts will come from, in some – though by no means all – cases via the chief executive posts in PCGs.

The other professions

There are brief references to the roles of health visitors in commissioning and a single mention of the other contractor professions (dentistry, pharmacy and optometry), with no real idea of how they fit in, because they do not. The flexibility of the NHS (Primary Care) Act 1997 is retained as the vehicle for developing primary and community services. This, together with the potential ability for primary care trusts to renegotiate the general medical services (GMS) contract locally, signals the possible end for independent contractor status in some areas. The persistent references to the retention of this status throughout the White Paper suggests that there is fire behind the smoke. However, the later guidance on the establishment of primary care trusts specifically refers to alternative models of providing personal medical services.

Herding cats

Quality and effectiveness also get a shove, in the form of promised indicators to assess the effectiveness of primary care at national and health authority level. Furthermore, each PCG will have to develop and promote clinical governance and professional development, with senior professional leadership at both group and practice level. This suggests a fairly low level of understanding by the authors of the White Paper of the dynamics of general practice. The evidence from new arrangements for GMS cover out of hours suggests that GPs can work together when it is in their own interests to do so. Peer review, however, is not part of the culture and introducing it is a much bigger step than reorganising the bureaucracy.

Not so fast and not so simple

Finally, there is a flash of recognition that undoing the eight years of fundholding in a period of 15 months from the publication of the White Paper may create some little local difficulty. For example, a high proportion of staff employed by practices under the fundholding scheme were effectively redundant and their skills were not required by the PCGs. Such affected staff include not only managers associated with the fundholding scheme, but also clinical staff – especially nurses – whose skills are still required but who only became affordable because of the management allowance for fundholding. Health authorities were required to set up clearing houses to manage these human resource issues and to minimise the employment impacts. Some authorities included only those staff directly associated with fundholding; others included all staff – mainly headquarters-based – who were affected by the totality of the changes taking place. The costs of redundancy had to be under-written by health authorities once the other potential sources (the remaining fundholder management allowance, accumulated savings from the fundholding scheme) had been exhausted.

The appointment of staff to the PCGs was a job for the board of the group, assisted by the health authority whose employer they remained. There remain a number of unresolved issues, such as what practices should do with the space occupied by former fundholding staff, often extensions paid for with savings from the fundholding scheme. The retained savings from the scheme (perhaps as much as £200 million nationally) are still owed to the practices who have a legal right to them. However, they must now seek the support of their PCG for their proposals to spend their savings. If such support is not forthcoming, a four-year programme of release of the resources (up to a maximum of £100 000) by the health authority to the practice is implemented.

Approaching equality

The allocation of integrated budgets to PCGs is a tool in the achievement of equality in the NHS. Initial allocations will be based on historical expenditure patterns in all the elements of the budget. Health authorities will develop a process for moving PCG budgets towards their equal shares of the national health budget over a period of time. The principles underlying these policies will be initial continuity and stability, the avoidance of any reduction in a group's budget in any year and the achievement of equity over time, the maximum time period not having yet been determined.

Chapter 6: NHS trusts: partnership and performance

Just following orders

Trusts are seen as the victims of the market rather than its creators. They are now given the opportunity to make good by focusing on quality and efficiency (Box 2.10). There is little new in this except clinical governance, still tantalisingly undefined until *A First Class Service* was published in June 1998 (Box 2.11), and the rules on openness already implemented.

Remarriage is on the cards

While retaining their independence as corporate organisations, NHS trusts must now work in local partnerships and can only use NHS funds for the collective NHS agenda, uniquely described in the HImP. This is a fundamental change in culture for many NHS trusts and not one which has necessarily come naturally. As

Box 2.10   A new paradigm for NHS trusts

- NHS trusts will participate in strategy and planning by helping shape the HImP

- New standards for quality and efficiency, explicit in local agreements (between health authorities, PCGs and NHS trusts) alongside new measures of efficiency

- Doctors, nurses and other senior professionals will be more closely involved in designing service agreements with commissioners, and in aligning NHS trust financial priorities with clinical priorities

- Clinical governance arrangements will be developed in all NHS trusts to guarantee an emphasis on quality

- NHS trusts will be able to share and invest efficiency gains to improve services consistent with the HImP

- Public confidence will be rebuilt through openness, improved governance and public commitment to the values and aims of the NHS

Box 2.11   Defining clinical governanace (from *A First Class Service*)

... a framework through which NHS organisations are accountable for continuously improving the quality of their services and safeguarding high standards of care by creating an environment in which excellence in clinical care will flourish

elsewhere, there is a boost for nursing as an independent profession with a distinctive contribution to make. The main thrust, however, is on quality and the most detailed account at this stage of clinical governance (Box 2.12).

> **Box 2.12 Characteristics of a quality organisation exercising clinical governance**
>
> - Quality improvement, e.g. clinical audit, is in place and integrated with the quality programme for the whole organisation
>
> - Leadership skills are developed for each clinical team
>
> - Evidence-based practice is in day-to-day use with infrastructure to support it
>
> - There is systematic dissemination (inside and outside the organisation) of evaluated good practice, ideas and innovations
>
> - High standards clinical risk reduction programmes are in place
>
> - Adverse events are detected, openly investigated; and the lessons learned are promptly applied
>
> - Lessons for clinical practice, from complaints by patients, are systematically learned
>
> - Poor clinical performance is recognised at an early stage and dealt with to prevent harm to patients
>
> - Professional development programmes reflect the principles of clinical governance
>
> - High-quality data are collected to monitor clinical care

Clinical quality first

Every NHS trust has to embrace the concept of clinical governance so that quality is at the core of their organisational and professional responsibilities. The 1999 Health Act gives NHS trusts a new duty for quality of care and their chief executives will carry ultimate responsibility for assuring the quality of care. Appropriate local arrangements, such as a board subcommittee led by a senior clinical professional, have been put in place to ensure the internal clinical governance of the organisation. These arrangements, which strengthen existing professional self-regulation, will gradually extend to engage professionals at ward and clinical team level. Monthly reports on quality are being presented to NHS trust boards together with an annual report. This is all very open and up front; it is also a manifestation of this government's favourite tool of control: naming, shaming and blaming. While there is a degree of moral superiority in the approach, it is hardly compatible with a statutory duty of partnership. Engaging professionals in their own public humiliation is not likely to be a popular strategy with the people who actually make up the NHS, the health professionals.

Sanctions galore

The performance management of NHS trusts, the tools for which are covered in more detail elsewhere in Parts 2 and 3, is also hard hitting. Trusts will be subject to a new, broadly based performance framework; accountability through service agreements; accountability to the NHS Executive for statutory quality and financial performance; accountability to health authorities for doing their bidding in the HImP; and a statutory duty of partnership; who would want to be a trust chief executive? Furthermore, for miscreants there is a new formal five-stage system for taking NHS

Box 2.13   Investigation and intervention for failing NHS trusts

1 Health authorities call in the NHS Executive Regional Offices when an NHS trust is failing to deliver against the HImP

2 NHS Executive Regional Offices will investigate where there may be a failure to comply with statutory duties

3 The CHI will be called in to investigate and report on problems

4 PCGs will be able to change their local service agreements where NHS trusts are failing to deliver

5 The Secretary of State can remove NHS trust boards

trusts to the brink of destruction (Box 2.13). In fact, the only new bit of this is the CHI. It must be rather reassuring to NHS trusts that the removal of services comes at the fourth level and just before the removal of the trust itself!

There has been serious concern at the accountability of NHS trusts to the Regional Offices of the NHS Executive for clinical governance and other aspects of quality when they are accountable to health authorities for health improvement. PCGs and primary care trusts will be accountable to health authorities for all these features of the new NHS. It was strongly argued that NHS trusts should also be accountable to health authorities for clinical governance, but the guidance published in March 1999 retained the proposals in *A First Class Service* that the line of account should be to the NHS Executive. Some regard this as an unsustainable position.

Lower management and procedure costs

Under the heading of efficiency, despite a lot of words, it is hard to find anything really encouraging for NHS trusts. In fact, it is difficult to find anything at all except cuts in costs. Procedure costs are now benchmarked and published as 'reference costs', management costs will be reduced by abolishing the transactions of the internal market and extra-contractual referrals (plus the unspoken but widely practised mergers), and managers will be able to focus on managing not bureaucracy; but they won't be managing integrated hospital and community services, a service model which is now officially frowned upon. New mergers are forbidden from joining acute hospital services and community services where they were previously separately managed.

The efficiency requirements placed on NHS trusts for the 1999/2000 Service and Financial Framework were based on the relative position of their reference costs, based on acute hospital services only. The level of efficiency required varied from 2% to 4.5% in the trust with the highest reference costs (Leeds Teaching Hospitals). Community-based NHS trusts were all expected to deliver 3% efficiency.

Looking after staff

The government wants to be seen as kinder to staff than its predecessor and there are a lot of positive words to this end. Various initiatives are described in Box 2.14. A big inherited problem, however, is the chaos which local pay determination has imposed on pay structures. To convert from local pay to national pay would bring two seriously unwanted problems. First, average pay would rise, leading to cuts in services; second, some staff would lose pay – after protection – leading to staff dissatisfaction. To avoid these risks, and because it doesn't know what to do, the government treats this as a long-term issue and the topic of discussions.

Greater involvement of staff, together with open meetings, more

---

Box 2.14   Involving staff in NHS trusts

- Moving towards national pay with meaningful local flexibility

- Action on issues which affect the quality of working lives of NHS staff

- Immediate priority to
  - minimise accidents at work
  - avoid violence at work
  - address stress from work
  - recognise and deal with racism
  - flexible, family-friendly employment policies
  - reasonable standards of food and accommodation for on-call doctors
  - enable staff to speak out when necessary without victimisation

- Involving staff in planning service developments and changes

- A taskforce on involving frontline staff in shaping new patterns of healthcare

- NHS trust boards will have to review regularly their success in involving staff

- Publication in NHS trust annual reports of their policy on staff involvement and the outcome of negotiations or initiatives

representative boards and the publication of information are all designed to help build public confidence in the structures and ethos of the NHS, confidence which was dented during the turbulent years around the previous reforms. It was not long, however, before turbulence returned to NHS industrial relations with discord over the phasing of the 1998/99 review body pay awards. Tension over the exchange of higher pay awards for jobs and a fightback against the continued erosion of its independence by the medical profession are both likely in the near future.

In the summer of 1998, the government's strategy for the NHS workforce, *Working Together*, was published (see later). Unlike the contemporary strategy on information, which was backed with senior ministerial announcements and lots of money, the workforce strategy appears to be a piece of bureaucracy with much less commitment to change things. However, the higher-than-expected pay award for nurses and therapists in 1999, accompanied by a squeezing of differentials in junior nurses, was partly funded by £100 million from the Modernisation Fund with threatening rumours that radical changes in the structure and productivity of the professions was expected.

A further minimal but symbolic positive note was sounded when the allocation of the Modernisation Fund available for mental health services was heavily biased towards staff training and development, a sign that more positive attitudes to the most threatened and abused staff group in all the NHS was at least possible.

Chapter 7: The national dimension: a one-nation NHS

Tough at the top

While one can understand the presentational importance of starting with local structures and working up to the centre, this isn't quite what has been offered. We are first offered a new strategic role for health authorities, then the new PCGs which take on some old health authority functions, then NHS trusts, with a new paradigm and limited emasculation; now for the DoH, pre-eminent as always.

Unified policies

The DoH, we are told, will integrate policy on public health, social care and the NHS so that there is a clear national framework for similar local development; great. The NHS Executive will develop and implement policy for the NHS; fine. Management costs for the DoH and the NHS Executive will be subject to the same rigour as those of the NHS; good. As fewer and larger health authorities emerge (a conclusion not yet actioned and currently in some doubt), the role of NHS Executive Regional Offices will need to be kept under review; this means they will either be abolished, with health authorities becoming the regions, or they will be reduced in number to, say, two or four. Either way, the impact on the centre will be profound. The worst outcome could be that health authorities are absorbed into the NHS Executive, replacing the Regional Offices, which would again deprive the operational NHS of any strategic role, increase the role of the civil service and reduce the career options for senior staff in the NHS.

NICE, CHI and NSFs

There is a national drive for quality and clinical effectiveness too, bearing down on unjustifiable variations in the application of evidence of clinical and cost-effectiveness (Box 2.15). This is a very strong framework if it can be realised. The R&D strategy is already in place, although there has been a long dispute over which branch of the NHS Executive has responsibility for the dissemination of the results of research. The NSFs are to be based on the cancer services model, which has proved to be a unifying force and has led to improvements in local services. The intention is to publish a further NSF each year; priorities for 1999 are mental health services and coronary heart disease, a framework for services for older people is being developed for 2000 and for diabetes in 2001. The

Box 2.15   The national initiative on clinical and cost effectiveness

- The R&D programme will ensure the provision and dissemination of high-quality scientific evidence on the cost-effectiveness and quality of care

- A programme of new evidence-based NSFs will set out patterns and levels of service which should be provided for patients with certain conditions

- The new NICE will promote clinical and cost-effectiveness by producing clinical guidelines and audits for dissemination throughout the NHS

- The new CHI will support and oversee the quality of clinical governance and of clinical services

- Work with the professions to strengthen existing systems of professional self-regulation

two new bodies are best known for their populist acronyms (NICE (Box 2.16) and CHI, formerly known as CHIMP).

The repeated references to cost-effectiveness may suggest that the government is really serious about making choices of priorities on the basis of the value of the benefits for patients. Indeed, the absence of any reference to comprehensiveness in all the descriptions of the new NHS suggest that the government may have privately acknowledged that some limitations of scope for tax-funded healthcare may well be necessary and it is putting in place the justification for the tough decisions which may well follow in the future. The licensing of Viagra (sildenafil), a cheap and effective treatment for male erectile dysfunction (impotence), bounced the government into action before these structures were in place. Its rather dithering response to unwanted advice on the merits of the drug (from the Standing Medical Advisory Committee) showed how challenging a rationing policy might prove to be.

This is an important discipline and would take the boldness and intellectual status of the government's approach into uncharted waters. The Commission, on the other hand, is more like an inspec-

---

Box 2.16   The National Institute for Clinical Excellence

- New coherence and prominence to information about clinical and cost-effectiveness

- It will produce and disseminate
  - clinical guidelines based on relevant evidence of clinical and cost-effectiveness
  - clinical audit methodologies and information on good practice in clinical audit

- Bring together work done by many professional organisations receiving DoH funding

- Work to a programme agreed with the DoH

- Funded from resources already committed to this work (actually overheads disinvested from Royal Colleges funding in 1997/98)

- Membership will be drawn from the health professions, the NHS, academics, health economists and patient interests

---

torate along the lines of OFSTED, though presumably on a much smaller scale. It appears, however, to have the same powers of naming and shaming as OFSTED and the Secretary of State will have the same range of powers over failing health services as David Blunkett has exercised over schools.

New powers for Regional Directors

There is no change in the accountability of health authorities and NHS trusts to Regional Offices of the NHS Executive, though the issues on which they are held to account will change as previously described and the relationship between health authorities and NHS trusts will increasingly resemble line management. For implementing the HImP, NHS trusts will be directly accountable to health authorities; for clinical governance they will be accountable to NHS Executive Regional Offices, but must satisfy health authorities that their arrangements are robust. The management arrangements in Regional Offices for the performance management of health authorities and NHS trusts have been integrated and conducted on an integrated patch basis.

The internal market arrangements whereby disputes between health authorities and NHS trusts, for example over activity and funding levels, have been reduced in status to the extent that these issues have to be resolved locally in almost all cases. (Previously, Regional Offices made arbitration judgements often without reference to the ability of the 'purchasers' to pay.) Informal arrangements whereby Regional Directors were involved in the appointment of chief executives of health authorities and NHS trusts have now been formalised, an important symbol of the integration of the NHS and of reduced independence for each of its quangos.

Protection for specialist regional services

NHS Executive Regional Offices now have a new responsibility in overseeing the means by which the commissioning of specialist hospital services is carried out by groups of commissioners. This is to ensure fair access to highly specialised services where one provider meets the needs of more than one health authority. There are already national specialist commissioning advisory group (NSCAG) arrangements in place for those services where one provider meets the needs of more than one region, such as high-security psychiatric hospitals (to be devolved to regional level from 2000 onwards and 1999 in shadow form), liver transplantation, complex cranio-facial surgery. The full range of services to be covered by these new regional arrangements was published at the end of 1998 after a consultation process. Some groups of health authorities are already working together to commission specialist regional services. They do so by building on commissioning expertise which they possess for their mainstream commissioning responsibilities. By 2001, health authorities will be much less heavily engaged in commissioning, so a different arrangement may be necessary. Specialised commissioning units may be set up in Regional Offices, as third party agencies or in one health authority acting on behalf of several authorities. In the longer term, despite current political antagonism, these specialist commissioning arrangements could be harmonised with the redrawing of health authority boundaries covering populations in excess of one million.

Chapter 8: Measuring progress: better every year

A new performance framework

The accountability of any body is limited by what is measured; the new performance framework sets out to define what it is important to do well and therefore what should be measured. The White Paper is less precise on the detail but further information has since been published as a consultation paper and the framework to be used in 1999/2000 was released in April 1999.

The six dimensions of success

The new framework has six dimensions (Box 2.17). This will provide a much more rounded measure of NHS performance, among the best of any public service, and much more relevant to what the public and the professions want. The difficulty is not with

---

Box 2.17   Six dimensions of the new national performance framework

- Health improvement
  - reflecting the overall aim of improving the general health of the population, influenced by many factors beyond the NHS
  - for example, changes in premature death rates, reflecting social and economic factors

- Fair access
  - the NHS contribution must offer fair access to health services in relation to need, irrespective of geography, class, ethnicity, age or sex
  - for example, ensuring that black and minority ethnic groups are not disadvantaged in terms of access

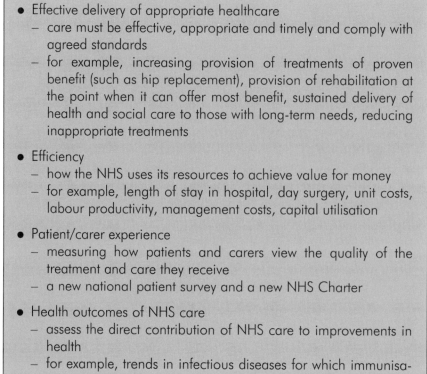

- Effective delivery of appropriate healthcare
  - care must be effective, appropriate and timely and comply with agreed standards
  - for example, increasing provision of treatments of proven benefit (such as hip replacement), provision of rehabilitation at the point when it can offer most benefit, sustained delivery of health and social care to those with long-term needs, reducing inappropriate treatments
- Efficiency
  - how the NHS uses its resources to achieve value for money
  - for example, length of stay in hospital, day surgery, unit costs, labour productivity, management costs, capital utilisation
- Patient/carer experience
  - measuring how patients and carers view the quality of the treatment and care they receive
  - a new national patient survey and a new NHS Charter
- Health outcomes of NHS care
  - assess the direct contribution of NHS care to improvements in health
  - for example, trends in infectious diseases for which immunisation is available

the intent, or the acceptance of the intent by the NHS, but with developing robust and reliable measures of the six dimensions. In the consultation paper published in January 1998, a suggested set of high-level indicators was outlined (Box 2.18). It is intended that the framework should be useful to, and used by:

- the general public – to inform them about their local NHS and to inform decisions about their own care
- NHS agencies (health authorities, NHS trusts and PCGs) – to inform and improve performance and to use in planning
- ministers and the NHS Executive – to drive improvements in the performance of health authorities and to demonstrate public accountability for the use of NHS resources.

Box 2.18 Proposed set of high-level performance indicators

- Health improvement
  - deaths from all causes (for people aged 15–64)
  - deaths from all causes (for people aged 65–74)
  - cancer registrations – the summation of age- and sex-standardised rates for the following cancers:
    - stomach
    - small intestine, colon, rectum, rectosigmoid junction, anus
    - trachea, bronchus and lung
    - malignant melanoma
    - non-melanoma skin cancer
    - female breast
    - cervix uteri

- Fair access
  - surgery rates – a composite indicator of elective surgery rates, consisting of age- and sex-standardised:
    - coronary artery bypass graft (CABG) and percutaneous transluminal coronary angioplasty (PTCA) rates
    - hip replacement rates (for those over 65)
    - knee replacement rates (for those over 65)
    - cataract replacement rates
  - conceptions below age 16 – measuring access to family planning services
  - people registered with a NHS dentist – percentage of population registered
  - early detection of cancer – a composite indicator, consisting of:
    - percent of target population screened for breast cancer
    - percent of target population screened for cervical cancer
  - district nurse contacts – a composite indicator looking at access to community services, consisting of:
    - district nurse contacts for those aged 75 and over
    - district nurse contacts over 30 minutes for those aged 75 and over
    - assisted district nurse contacts for those aged 75 and over

- Effective delivery of appropriate healthcare
  - disease prevention and health promotion – a composite indicator consisting of:
    - percent of target population vaccinated
    - percent of all orchidopexies below age 5
  - early detection of cancer – a composite indicator of breast and cervical cancer screening as above
  - inappropriately used surgery – a composite indicator consisting of age- and sex-standardised:
    - rates of Ds & Cs performed in women under 40
    - surgical intervention rates for glue ear
  - surgery rates – a composite indicator of elective surgery rates for CABG, PTCA, hip and knee replacement and cataract replacement as above
  - acute care management – a composite indicator consisting of age- and sex-standardised admission rates for:
    - severe ENT infection
    - kidney/urinary tract infection
    - heart failure
  - chronic care management – a composite indicator consisting of age- and sex-standardised admission rates for:
    - asthma
    - diabetes
    - epilepsy
  - mental health in primary care – a composite indicator consisting of:
    - volume of benzodiazepines
    - ratio of antidepressants to benzodiazepines prescribed
  - cost effective prescribing – a composite measure consisting of:
    - cost/ASTRO-PU of combination products
    - cost/ASTRO-PU of modified release products
    - cost/ASTRO-PU of drugs of limited clinical value
    - cost/ASTRO-PU of inhaled corticosteroids
  - discharge from hospital – a composite indicator consisting of:
    - rate of discharge home within 56 days of emergency admission from home with a stroke
    - rate of discharge home within 56 days of admission with a fractured neck of femur

- Efficiency
  - day case rate
  - length of stay in hospital (case-mix adjusted)
  - unit cost (Hospital and Community Health Services)
  - generic prescribing (%)

- Patient/carer experience of the NHS
  - patients who wait more than 2 hours for emergency admission (admitted through A&E)
  - patients with operations cancelled for non-medical reasons on the day of, or after, admission
  - delayed discharge from hospital for people aged over 75 (per 1000 75-year-olds not in hospital)
  - first outpatient appointments for which patient did not attend (%)
  - outpatients seen within 13 weeks of GP referral (%)
  - inpatients admitted within 3 months of a decision to admit (%)

- Health outcomes of NHS care
  - conceptions below age 16
  - decayed, missing and filled teeth in 5-year-olds
  - avoidable diseases – a composite indicator of avoidable diseases and impairments, consisting of age- and sex-standardised:
    - notification rates for pertussis in children
    - notification rates for measles
    - episode rates for fracture of proximal femur (in those aged 65 and over)
    - notification rates for TB
  - adverse events/complications of treatment – a composite indicator consisting of age-standardised:
    - 28-day emergency admission rates
    - rates of surgery for hernia recurrence
  - emergency admissions to hospital for people aged over 75 (per 1000 75-year-olds)
  - emergency psychiatric readmission rate
  - infant deaths – a composite indicator consisting of:
    - stillbirth rates
    - infant mortality rates

- survival rates for breast and cervical cancer – a composite indicator of five-year survival rates consisting of age- (and sex-) standardised:
  - survival rates from breast cancer (ages 50–69)
  - survival rates from cervical cancer (ages 15–74)
- avoidable deaths – a composite indicator of potentially avoidable deaths consisting of
  - peptic ulcer (ages 25–74)
  - fracture of skull and intracranial injury (ages 1+)
  - maternal deaths (ages 15–44)
  - tuberculosis (ages 5–64)
  - Hodgkin's disease (ages 5–64)
  - chronic rheumatic heart disease (ages 5–44)
  - hypertensive and cerebrovascular disease (ages 35–64)
  - asthma (ages 5–44)
  - appendicitis, abdominal hernia, cholelithiasis and cholecystitis (ages 5–64)
  - coronary heart disease (ages under 65)

Better but not perfect

The list includes indicators for primary care practice and clinical effectiveness, clinical indicators for hospital practice and indicators for health authorities who will be held to account for delivering the whole package. Consultation exercises were conducted during 1997 on the clinical and primary care indicators and, during 1998, on the full list of high-level indicators. Road testing of the proposed indicators has been carried out but doubt persists about the validity and usefulness of many of the indicators. The list is not, and never will be, perfect, but significant progress is being made in defining the appropriate products of healthcare in a comprehensive system. Unfortunately, as with previous efforts at judging performance, these indicators are focused on acute hospital activity and are relatively biased against community-based services. At present, no suitable measures exist for integrated care in the community or for continuing care; this reflects the traditional lack of emphasis on, and information about, these sectors. A separate set of indicators has subsequently been published for the assessment of social services performance and efforts have been made to integrate local assessments of services across sectors.

Few of the proposed indicators offer anything new, although they have not been used to performance manage health authorities before. Some of the indicators, such as notification rates, are worthless as they have no scientific validity or consistency. Others, such as cervical cancer (survival), cover events which are so rare as to be meaningless at local level over periods of less than ten years. Others, especially those based on acute hospital activity, are based on incomplete and inaccurate data collected for other purposes. Nonetheless, unless measures such as these are used to change the way the NHS is managed, no effort will be put into improving the ones now on offer. Necessity may prove to be the mother of invention.

There is full recognition of the poverty of knowledge about what patients want and think. The national survey of patient and user experience is announced, with the promise that analysis of the results will be possible at individual health authority level. It is not yet known whether it will be possible to differentiate between smaller areas such as those to be covered by PCGs. The first survey, starting in October 1998, is a general questionnaire of 100 000 patients in general practice. An extension of the survey in 1999 will concentrate on patients in hospital with cancer or heart disease. Again, we see no specific attention paid to the public's highest priority of mental health. There is growing concern among health scientists that this government, like others, uses statistics to prove what it wants but rejects statistical analysis to explain variations. Most variations at local level are not statistically significant; it would be wrong to change policy on the basis of such findings.

Chapter 9: How the money will flow: from red tape to patient care

How, not how much?

What should have been the most interesting, informative and crucial chapter for most NHS staff and observers turns out to be the most dull. In the absence of cabinet agreement at the time, prior to the result of the Comprehensive Spending Review, on the future of NHS funding, all that is offered is a critique of the old system of distributing funds and an outline of the approach to the new system. The basic problem facing the government was that the internal market was the means by which funds allocated by parliament reached the point of expenditure on patient care. To replace the internal market, without returning to the monopolies of 1990, has tested the government's ingenuity. The chosen solution, allocation to PCGs which then allocate to NHS trusts through long-term service agreements, is a reasonable compromise between the historical structures but carries new risks of its own.

Quality, not money, following patients

The key changes have been described in earlier chapters, including unifying budgets in PCGs, flexible use of these resources, stability through long-term agreements, benchmarking costs of NHS trusts and reducing bureaucracy. Two additional changes are proposed: a new allocation formula, which, although not specified at this level, will give greater weight to inner-city deprivation; and a revised approach to major capital schemes using the regenerated PFI and putting clinical needs at the top of the criteria list for prioritising building schemes. Later, with the PFI continuing to disappoint, more public capital investment became available. The previous government's reforms sought to ensure that money followed patients in the health system; it worked only up to a point and it stopped working when the money ran out. While the underlying principles (freedom of movement for patients and reward for good services) remain valid, penalising substandard performance with financial leverage is to be replaced by mechanisms which raise poor performance so that, in common with the Calman–Hine principles for cancer services, care of high and even quality is available to all.

Collective responsibility and risk sharing

There is a strong push for the development and value of longer-term agreements, and NHS trusts are given a share of the responsibility for ensuring that activity does not get out of kilter with funding, one of the drivers for the current and episodic insolvency of the NHS. GPs will continue to have the freedom to refer and to prescribe the drugs that patients need, within the overall budget of the PCG but without the bureaucracy of the extra-contractual referral system. This will be replaced, as far as NHS providers are concerned, by the incorporation of historical patient flows into service agreements and the development of an annual review of patient flows feeding into financial allocations, through health authorities, two years in arrears. This system, known as 'OATS' (out of area treatments) applies to NHS trusts only; for private sector providers, the extra-contractual referral system is still in use. There will be a significant reduction in paperwork associated with the new system and relative financial stability for trusts.

More management but at less cost

The drive to reduce expenditure on management and administration has been a cause célèbre of successive governments. NHS management costs go in cycles; rising in 1974, falling in 1982; rising at the end of the 1980s and early 1990s and falling again since 1994. The current round of reductions will lead to an overall reduction in management costs as a proportion of total NHS expenditure of the order of 0.7% between 1997 and 2002. The main means of doing so, while retaining competent management, are outlined in Box 2.19. It is also believed by many, including politicians, that organisational mergers will release resources from management overheads. This

---

Box. 2.19   Cutting bureaucracy in *The new NHS*

- Ending the internal market will reduce bureaucracy by:
  - replacing the annual contracting round with long term agreements
  - abolishing extra-contractual referrals and cost-per-case contracts
  - moving from GP fundholding to inclusive PCGs
  - reshaping health authorities with savings in core administration (independent contractor services) allowing reinvestment in their new role
  - ending competition and bearing down on NHS trust management and administrative costs generated by the internal market
  - integrating primary care and community trusts
  - sharing support functions between NHS organisations

---

can be an illusion unless the reduction in management costs is a *sine qua non* for the merger. The belief is likely to be sorely tested during the current frenetic round of mergers.

After 1999, a line has been drawn under management costs for health authorities and PCGs. In addition, a range of management activities in areas of priority to the government, such as public health and prescribing controls, are now exempted from official measurement of management costs. With such a massive programme of change management, there is a genuine risk that the NHS will become undermanaged in a way that starts to compromise effectiveness. Subsequent mergers of PCGs and trusts and of NHS trusts and possibly health authorities will generate further savings in management costs during the next five years. However, over-centralisation will inevitably lead to the creation of smaller local structures in future years which will impose a new burden on NHS management resources.

Chapter 10: Making it happen: rolling out change

An agenda for action

This final chapter lays out the early actions by this government in implementing changes to the NHS. Early milestones are signalled in Box 2.20 and actions already taken by the time of publication of the White Paper are described in Box 2.21. Overall, there was a hint of optimism and a great deal of determination. The believability of the strategy is dented only by the claim that the White Paper will not lead to a wholesale reorganisation when we have already seen that such an outcome is inevitable, due to the radicalism of the proposals as well as the games that NHS managers like to play. The population health targets set by the public health strategy are integrated better with the planning process than the *Health of the Nation* could ever be with the internal market. *Our Healthier Nation* is also better focused on primary care, which was almost completely bypassed by its predecessor.

Box 2.20   Early milestones

1998

- three telephone advice helplines set up (staffed by nurses)

- projects established to demonstrate the benefits of the NHSnet

- a new information management and technology strategy for the NHS to be published

- consultation documents on quality and performance issues

- public health Green Paper *Our Healthier Nation* issues

- HAZs begin

- a new NHS Charter

- the first national survey of users and carers

- health authorities begin work with partner organisations on prototype HImPs for 1999

- GP Commissioning Pilots begin

- development work on PCGs, on new financial arrangements and on new performance indicators

1999

- introduction of two-week waiting time limit for urgent suspected breast cancer

- new PCGs begin, subsuming GP fundholding

- new statutory duties on partnership, health and quality

- development of local clinical governance, the new NICE and CHI

- new unified local health budgets for hospital and community services (commissioning), GP prescribing and the general practice infrastructure

- new funding arrangements for NHS trusts in place

Box 2.21   Early action on the six key principles

- action to raise standards across the country in breast cancer services and paediatric care, in a single national health service

- announcement of new HAZs to explore new, flexible, local ways of delivering health and healthcare

- a new approach to partnership in the NHS for the 1998/99 commissioning round

- action to improve efficiency by reducing management costs

- action teams to tackle inherited rising waiting lists and times, improving performance across the country

- rebuilding public confidence by opening NHS trust board meetings to the public and launching consultation on a new NHS Charter

HAZ and HAZ-nots

Health Action Zones remain obscure in their uniqueness; do they offer any more than a particular model of multiagency approaches to health and the integration of health and social care? It was intended that the HAZ model would be used initially to provide the framework for major hospital building and restructuring schemes using the PFI, for embracing the wider public health agenda in deprived areas, and as part of local regeneration projects including Single Regeneration Budget (SRB) proposals and European Union initiatives. I suspect that the approach originally described in the HAZ trailer became adopted as the norm before this White Paper was completed, hence the fairly downbeat presentation of HAZs here. Everyone will be doing it, but only a select few will get the badge and the T-shirt.

A further gimmick in this area is the establishment of Healthy Living Centres, taking advantage of the New Opportunities Fund, an additional special fund benefiting from proceeds from the National Lottery. Identified as a government intention as early as December 1997, but not able to be implemented until after legislation to change the way lottery funds are used, Healthy Living Centres are designed to be a focus for community-based action to improve health and reduce inequalities. There is no evidence to support these initiatives but there is no evidence to reject them either. They are seen as providing an opportunity to mobilise community activity to achieve these ends, to provide a focus for health promotion in its broadest sense and to improve access to mainstream services. Up to a total of £232.5 million is available to authorities in England for these centres, with funding for each scheme available for up to five years. It is intended to commit two thirds of the money by 2001. It is expected that the HAZs will be best placed to succeed in securing a Healthy Living Centre, although smaller deprived communities in other areas may also benefit.

The HImP enshrines the basic principles of HAZs but expects them to be applied by all NHS organisations. In reality, the HAZ initiative is unnecessary except as a vehicle to direct funding to particular areas of need or political sensitivity. As a means of forcing health and local authorities to break down their traditional barriers, the HAZ initiative may prove to be ground-breaking but the greatest progress may well be made in areas of lesser need and/or where cross-agency relationships have traditionally been better developed.

Do I perceive realism?

In summary, this is the first long-term structural strategy for the NHS for a quarter of a century. It has many strengths and time to iron out the weaknesses. The biggest obstacle is the full engagement of the professions in the initial structures; where are the incentives? However, the government does recognise that some changes take time while others will be pushed harder in the short term, a sense of realism which is heartening.

Part 3

The Health Improvement Programme

Introduction

The Health Improvement Programme (HImP) is the embodiment of the new partnership in public services, which is the hallmark of the government's expectations of managers in the public sector. It is, in a way, a reaction to the fragmentation caused by the NHS internal market and the long-standing barriers which have compromised the effectiveness of combined health and social services initiatives. Having set itself against a radical reorganisation of health and local authorities, to avoid the dysfunction and political fallout which would result, the alternative strategy is to ensure that the benefits of integrated services are achieved without these problems. It is therefore expected that health authorities will coordinate the activities of the whole of the public sector in a unified effort to improve the health of the population and to raise the quality of services.

An added value philosophy

By planning action for health together, and by doing their normal activities in a much broader context created by multiagency strategies, authorities will find that every action has a higher value than when it is planned and delivered in an isolated context. This philosophy underpins the principles of the HImP. The overarching political ambition envisages that separate agencies will plan services together, and deliver services in complementary partnerships, to improve health and personal care by creating and using new networks in order to build a fairer and more equitable society in which the technical advances enjoyed by our society are appropriately combined with caring values and practices so that all citizens may benefit equally.

This long-term vision, which even this government acknowledges may take some time to attain (hence the ten-year plan), is to be converted into reality by a systematic series of steps which commit both central government and local agencies to change the way they have worked in the past. Although ambitious and complex in its scope and scale, the HImP enterprise builds on recent success in terms of a set of initiatives to manage winter pressures on services by planning and implementing innovative services on a whole-systems basis, ignoring the traditional boundaries of organisations, professions, funding responsibilities and government department accountability.

A timescale for development

The first attempt at producing a HImP was not expected to be mature, complete or long term. However, by April 1999, health authorities were expected to have established the networks and mechanisms for developing a comprehensive HImP by 2002 for the period to 2005. The minimum expectations of the first HImPs were described in October 1998 guidance (Box 3.1).

From these early beginnings a comprehensive programme will gradually emerge, increasingly informed by national imperatives and priorities and rising expectations in terms of performance and

Box 3.1 The first Health Improvement Programmes

These will:

- build on existing local planning

- (begin to) respond to the National Priorities Guidance and the NHS Modernisation Fund

- (begin to) set a strategic framework for action on national and local priorities, including the four *Our Healthier Nation* priorities, and reducing local health inequalities

- plan the local response to the NSFs for coronary heart disease and mental health and the existing Calman–Hine programme (on cancer)

- (begin to) address the commitment to modernise the NHS and how to meet the objectives in the National Priorities Guidance and for the NHS Modernisation Fund

- include Joint Investment Plans for older people

- include a Service and Financial Framework for the NHS, including the allocation of resources (to NHS trusts) to meet the national and local priorities

- describe the process for developing the HImP and how greater involvement will be developed in the future

delivery of radical change. The HAZs, introduced in two waves during 1998, were designed to tackle health inequalities, reshape services to better meet local needs and develop new approaches to partnership working. Try as I have, I am unable to differentiate this from the universal requirements of the HImP. I reluctantly conclude that the HAZ initiative was merely a means of diverting funds preferentially to inner cities in addition to the redistribution encouraged by the new formula introduced in 1999 for the allocation of the single budget to health authorities.

Health authorities, leading and shaping

The HImP is drafted on the basis of health authority populations. Wider communities, such as those covered by multiauthority HAZs, and local groupings, such as PCGs, will also be covered by HImPs and, in due course, the programmes will have sufficient flexibility to subanalyse by all definable population groups. However, whatever variations are introduced in the future, the mandatory framework for the HImP will continue to be the health authority, which will retain the statutory coordinating and other important functions (Box 3.2).

Box 3.2   HImPs: the responsibilities of health authorities

- to provide strategic leadership and coordination of the development and involvement of the HImP and to ensure the involvement of all stakeholders including users of services and their carers

- to ensure the delivery of the NHS responsibilities within the HImP, which are allocated to NHS trusts and to PCGs trusts

- to ensure that the NHS agencies support local authorities and other partners in the delivery of their responsibilities contained within the HImP

These responsibilities greatly enhance the status of health authorities relative to NHS trusts and clearly establish them as the senior partner in the local NHS. While NHS trusts remain accountable to NHS Executive Regional Offices, it is increasingly to health authorities that they look for agreement to their intentions and aspirations. These changes especially apply to the use of capital by NHS trusts, hitherto a private arrangement between them and the NHS Executive, now a public agreement with the health authority.

The policy context

The energetic new ministers of the Blair government have succeeded in swamping their departments with initiatives of greater or lesser importance. To their authors, of course, they are all that matters, until they are moved to another department or brief. The NHS and its main partners in local government have gradually become overwhelmed by these ministerial initiatives, at a time when – in the NHS at least – investment in management capacity has been steadily reduced.

For accommodation within the HImP are a set of complex policy frameworks for the NHS, for social services, other components of local government and wider governmental initiatives (Box 3.3).

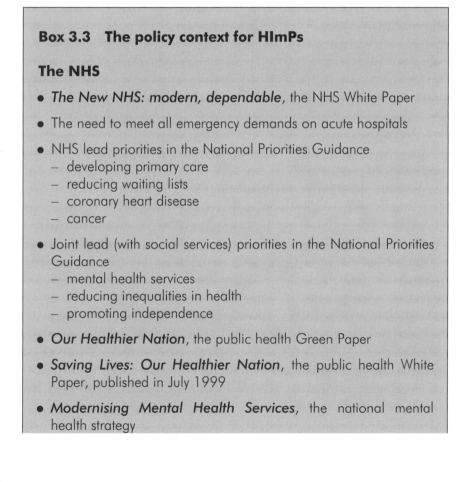

Box 3.3   The policy context for HImPs

The NHS

- *The New NHS: modern, dependable*, the NHS White Paper

- The need to meet all emergency demands on acute hospitals

- NHS lead priorities in the National Priorities Guidance
  - developing primary care
  - reducing waiting lists
  - coronary heart disease
  - cancer

- Joint lead (with social services) priorities in the National Priorities Guidance
  - mental health services
  - reducing inequalities in health
  - promoting independence

- *Our Healthier Nation*, the public health Green Paper

- *Saving Lives: Our Healthier Nation*, the public health White Paper, published in July 1999

- *Modernising Mental Health Services*, the national mental health strategy

- *Information for Health*, the strategy for information and communications technology for the NHS

- *Working Together*, the human resources strategy for the NHS

- NSFs for cancer, mental health and coronary heart disease

- *Smoking Kills*, the White Paper on tobacco control (also applies to wider government agenda)

Social services

- Social services lead priorities in the National Priorities Guidance
  - children's welfare
  - inter-agency working
  - regulation

- *Modernising Social Services*, the social services White Paper

- *Quality Protects*, a White Paper to help vulnerable children and young people

- The national carers strategy

- *Better Services for Vulnerable People*, leading to Joint Investment Plans

- *Partnership in Action*, a Green Paper on joint working at the interface between health and social services

Wider government

- *Modern Local Government: in touch with the people*, a White Paper introducing radical changes into the role and structure of local councils

- *A New Deal for Transport: better for everyone*, a national integrated transport strategy including aspects of air safety

- *Tackling Drugs to Build a Better Britain*, a White Paper on drugs control and treatment

- A New Deal on employment, funded through the windfall tax on privatised public utilities

- The Crime and Disorder Act, 1998, establishing community safety strategies and Youth Offending Teams
- A wide range of initiatives in schools and education, including pre-school strategies such as 'Early Years'
- The Social Exclusion Unit

Central to the task of converting policy into action is the National Priorities Guidance for Health and Social Services published in September 1998. For the ten priority areas described in the guidance, detailed targets are set for the short term, but the most important aspect of the guidance is the fact that it combines health and social care at the policy, strategy and implementation level for the first time.

The onward march of ministerial ambitions is creating initiative fatigue throughout the public services. With increasing complexity of the networks and stakeholders, and the introduction of real user empowerment in its infancy, the feasibility of delivering a comprehensive programme of change which has universal support and ownership and can address the whole of the policy framework to ministers' satisfaction is decreasingly probable. It remains to be seen how willing the government is to compromise its pace of ambition in the face of the evidence of the accelerating exhaustion of its servants.

The key strategic themes

An attempt to manage the scale of this agenda requires some constants. The adoption of key strategic themes, which run through the whole programme and across all the policy drivers, enables the development of an evolutionary HImP, building on core programmes and helping to capture partners in the process. Below are described the main strategic drivers for health improvement which should inform and harness action to improve health (Box 3.4).

> **Box 3.4   Key strategic themes for health improvement**
>
> • public health and inequalities in health
>
> • range and location of services
>
> • medium-term financial strategy
>
> • national framework for assessing performance
>
> • involving patients and the public

Public health and inequalities in health

Having eventually released its Green Paper on public health, the government could be quietly pleased with its reception. Compared with its predecessor, *Health of the Nation*, the Green Paper had a much tighter focus, a more open approach to ownership, leadership and responsibility and, most important of all, a recognition of the vital interrelationship between poverty and ill health. *Our Healthier Nation* was a consultation document on which views were sought. It was, however, relatively mature in its conception and the shape of the national strategy for health was already clearly visible. With a consultation period of less than three months and publication of the subsequent White Paper intended shortly afterwards, the die was cast, although in the event, the traumas within the DoH which delayed the Green Paper also held up completion of the White Paper, published with little pomp 17 months later.

In addition to clearly stated aims (Box 3.5) and targets (Box 3.6), the basic currency of the strategy was a set of tripartite contracts between the government, management agencies (such as health authorities, local authorities, schools or employers) and the people. The contract was outlined for the strategy as a whole, for each target and for each of three key settings in which action was required: schools – for children; workplaces – for adults; and neighbourhoods – for elderly people.

These are interesting policies, representing major changes in strategy and approach to the health of the population. It would be wrong and grossly unfair to criticise the previous government for

Box 3.5 **The government's key aims in *Our Healthier Nation***

- To improve the health of the population as a whole by increasing the length of people's lives and the number of years people spend free from illness

- To improve the health of the worst off in society and to narrow the health gap

Box 3.6 **National health targets in *Saving Lives: Our Healthier Nation***

By the year 2010 (baseline year the average of 1996, 1997 and 1998):

- **heart disease** and **stroke**: to reduce the death rate from heart disease, stroke and related illnesses among people aged under 75 years by at least **40%**

- **accidents**: to reduce deaths from accidents by at least **a fifth** and serious injuries by **10%**

- **cancer**: to reduce the death rate from cancer among people aged under 75 years by at least **a fifth**

- **mental health**: to reduce the death rate from suicide and undetermined injury by **a fifth**

Health of the Nation, flawed though it was, as it constituted the first attempt in modern times to focus attention on population level health gain. *Saving Lives: Our Healthier Nation* should be seen as improving and redirecting the national strategy for health; the special characteristics being a focus on preventing premature death (under the age of retirement at 65), reducing inequalities in health, and reducing the duration of illness and disability. Only the first of these is likely to be achieved but there will be a good deal of attention on the attempts to pursue the others and success is not out of the question.

Moving targets

Although there are superficial similarities between the new targets and the old, there are more profound and important differences. The key areas are the same, except for the dropping of sexual health, which is to be addressed in a separate policy White Paper, also delayed for unexplained reasons. The targets for reducing death rates in the Green Paper focused on cardiovascular disease and stroke and cancer in under 65-year-olds for whom they account for two thirds of all deaths. The far more numerous deaths in 65–74-year-old people which featured in *Health of the Nation* were restored after consultation. It could be argued that they were chosen simply for the sake of it without any clear goal other than measurement, whereas the Green Paper target, backed by the drive on inequalities, set out to achieve an increase in survivors beyond working age, to enjoy the fruits of retirement. The behavioural targets in *Health of the Nation* have also been dropped, mainly because they were unattainable but also because they were pointless, it being health outcomes that constituted their purpose. The greatest weakness of the previous government's strategy was their unwillingness to take action to support their own targets, especially in tobacco and alcohol consumption. The present government remains 'on approval' in this regard but a White Paper on tobacco control (*Smoking Kills*) was published late in 1998. The target for accidents replaces several targets focused on different age groups. Accidents in children and in elderly people display very high social class differentials; reducing these excesses in poor people would be a prime example of success in the fight against social exclusion. Accidental deaths in young adults, a *Health of the Nation* target, reflect car usership and are more common in affluent and rural settings. The least robust, and most disappointing, target – and therefore likely to come in for most criticism – is that for suicide. The targeting of suicide assumes that suicide is wrong and avoidable, that it can be prevented by health service and other community action and that it can be reliably measured. In fact, suicide can be a rational action by a distressed but not mentally ill person; unlike observations in the 1960s, most suicides, especially young men – the group causing most concern – do not seek medical help shortly before the act; coroner's court verdicts can appear to be based on the interests of the family rather than the facts. Measurement will prove to be a major challenge for these targets.

Factor analysis

The Green and White Papers will be widely used by students as a source for statistics on health inequalities and trends in health performance. It is rather surprising that so few copies were made available to the NHS; the whole papers were available on the DoH website but graphs and figures do not download well and the original in colour is required to make presentations. They also included an intelligent analysis of the factors which affect health (Box 3.7). Special attention is given to the impact of unemployment on early death, the consequences of smoking, ethnicity and social class variations.

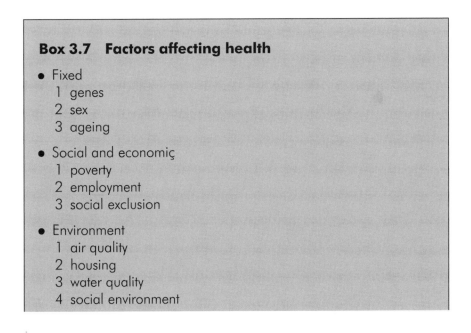

Box 3.7   Factors affecting health

- Fixed
  1 genes
  2 sex
  3 ageing
- Social and economic
  1 poverty
  2 employment
  3 social exclusion
- Environment
  1 air quality
  2 housing
  3 water quality
  4 social environment

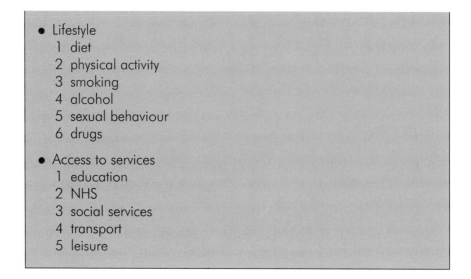

- Lifestyle
  1 diet
  2 physical activity
  3 smoking
  4 alcohol
  5 sexual behaviour
  6 drugs
- Access to services
  1 education
  2 NHS
  3 social services
  4 transport
  5 leisure

Contracts for health

The scene is set by the overall contract for health. There is also a contract for each of the four priority areas and for each setting. For each contract, the possible actions of the government are listed alongside those for local organisations and for the relevant group of people. Typical examples are given in Box 3.8.

The national contracts for the four priority areas cover four discrete factors as well as the three constituencies for action. These factors are social and economic, environmental, lifestyle and services. An example for heart disease and stroke is shown in Box 3.9.

Local choice

In addition to the four national priority areas, HImPs are expected to include a limited range of additional local priorities reflecting local communities and the issues which concern them. The Green Paper suggested some local priorities. It is clear that the scope for local prioritisation is limited given the very high political leadership of the whole agenda and the growing list of national priorities and

Box 3.8   Examples of the national contracts

A contract for health

- Government
  tackle the root causes of ill health

- Communities
  plan and provide high quality services to everyone who needs them

- People
  take responsibility for their own health and make healthier choices about their lifestyle

Healthy schools

- Government
  set high educational standards

- Schools
  give children the capacity to make the most of their lives and their future families' lives

- Pupils and parents
  work together to share responsibility for academic achievement, healthier eating, better exercise, and a responsible attitude to smoking, drugs, alcohol, sex and relationships

Healthy workplaces

- Government
  ensure minimum employment rights to encourage decent and responsible partnerships between staff and managers

- Employers
  take measures to reduce stress at work

- Employees
  support colleagues who have problems or who are disabled

Box 3.9   Examples of action to help achieve the target for heart disease and stroke

	Government and national players can	Local players and communities can	People can
Social and economic	continue to make smoking cost more through taxation	provide incentives to employees to cycle or walk to work, or leave their cars at home	take opportunities to better their lives through education, training and employment
Environmental	encourage employers to provide a smoke-free environment for non-smokers	through local employers and staff, work in partnership to reduce stress at work	protect others from second-hand smoke
Lifestyle	end advertising and promotion of cigarettes	encourage the development of healthy schools and healthy workplaces	stop smoking or cut down, watch what they eat and take regular exercise
Services	encourage doctors and nurses to give advice on healthier living	provide help to people who want to stop smoking	have their blood pressure checked regularly

imperatives. Indeed, the White Paper lists a number of additional national strategies in public health (Box 3.10).

Final thoughts on the Green Paper

Our Healthier Nation is destined to become an enigma. The flaws in the process of its introduction, and the impression the paper gives that it was written by a committee, detract from its many strengths. It describes the problems of inequality in the context of steady overall improvements in health (in general) and places a clear focus on where, how and by whom improvements need to be made. It is, perhaps, a little idealistic in terms of the language of the contract; it

---

Box 3.10   Possible local priorities and targets and new national strategies

Local

- Asthma and other respiratory problems

- Teenage pregnancy

- Infant mortality

- Back pain, rheumatism and arthritis

- Environment

- Diabetes

- Oral health

- Vulnerable groups

National

- Sexual health

- Drugs and alcohol

- A Food Standards Agency

- Water fluoridation

- Communicable disease prevention and control

- Genetics and health

---

is far more likely that the public expects the government to fulfil its part of the bargain than the government expects the public to fulfil its side. Nonetheless, as a consultation paper, with time during 1998 and 1999 for its focus and targets to be clarified in a White Paper of the same name, it provided a sound basis for the improvements in the health of the community which the affluence of the millennium ought to deliver for the whole community.

Reducing inequalities in health

Mapping inequalities in health has been an academic exercise for almost a century. Converting this knowledge into action to reduce inequalities in health has attracted less commitment and startlingly little success. Indeed, recent evidence assessed by the former Chief Medical Officer Sir Donald Acheson, on behalf of the government in preparation for the White Paper *Saving Lives: Our Healthier*

Box 3.11　What the NHS can do to reduce inequalities in health

- Provide equitable access to effective care in relation to need. This should be a governing principle of all NHS policies, including clinical governance, NICE guidelines, service frameworks to address inequity of access and performance management to focus on equitable access, and all NHS agencies should agree priorities for reducing inequity in access as part of the HImP

- Give priority to the achievement of more equitable allocation of NHS resources including:
  - helping health authorities furthest from target to move fastest towards their target allocation
  - extend needs-based weighting to GMS funding
  - review the formula for allocating funds for hospital and community health services to promote specific action to reduce inequalities through health promotion and public health action
  - review the relationship of private practice to the NHS with special reference to access to effective care, resource allocation and staff availability

- Directors of public health, on behalf of health and local authorities, should produce an equity profile for their population and undertake a triennial audit of progress towards reducing inequalities in health

- As part of health impact assessment, all policies likely to have an effect on health should be evaluated for their effect on inequalities and formulated in a way to favour the less well off

Nation, suggests that inequalities have grown since the substantive analysis by Sir Douglas Black in 1980. In most cases, however, such analyses are self-fulfilling because the subclassification of the population – for example by social class – is redesigned periodically to amplify the differences between groups. Both the Black report and the Acheson analysis identified various proposals to reduce inequalities in health; Acheson also makes proposals for specific NHS action (Box 3.11) to reduce inequalities in health, and also in other domains, such as education, tax and benefits, employment, mobility, transport and pollution, nutrition and agriculture (including reform to the Common Agricultural Policy), for different age groups and ethnic minorities and, finally, to combat gender discrimination. Given that health experience is a moving target, it is difficult to be certain how effective individual or combined actions will be. A targeted research programme is being funded by the government to assess these impacts.

The clear intention of the government, outlined in the National Priorities Guidance for 1999–2002, is to improve the health of the

---

Box 3.12   Objectives for reducing health inequalities

- Address particular local inequalities, such as unwanted teenage conceptions and fair access to services for minority groups and socially excluded people

- Reduce accidents by 20% in children, young people and older people by 2010 (an *Our Healthier Nation* target and one which especially focuses on the most disadvantaged)

- Work towards smoking cessation policies (especially providing smoking cessation services for the least well-off)

- Improve provision of effective treatment for drug misusers (to reduce social exclusion – part of the *Tackling Drugs to Build a Better Britain* strategy and supported by the Modernisation Fund) and increase the uptake of hepatitis B immunisation among drug users

- Maintain or raise childhood immunisation rates to 95% (health authority-based statistics)

worst-off in society at a faster rate than the rest of the population. A set of key objectives, loosely based on the Acheson ideas, is included in the guidance and forms part of the mandatory HImP content for the first year (1999/2000) although the outcomes are many years in the future (Box 3.12).

For each specialist programme within the HImP, the inequalities issue needs to be addressed, both in terms of access to effective services and with regard to the rate of improvement in health outcomes. The ambition to make faster progress in health experience for the most disadvantaged is noble but extremely challenging, an outcome only seen during times of national hardship (wartime and recession). It is to tackle this challenge that HAZs have been established in areas with high levels of disadvantage and poor health experience. Twenty six HAZs have now been set up, covering almost one third of England; half are in the north of the country and only five in the south east. This distribution reflects the health of the people and their needs.

A further feature of inequality, which has emerged following the enquiry into the death of Stephen Lawrence and the carnage of the reputation of the police force which ensued, is that of discrimination. Whether it is on grounds of race, religion, gender, age, nationality, class or diagnosis, discrimination is damaging to social performance including health. All public services have a special responsibility to identify and eradicate discrimination. Paradoxically, organisations which behave with institutional discrimination will automatically deny that they discriminate negatively; organisations which are sensitive to individual needs and interests will continually strive to improve and address their real or potential weaknesses. Thus, one must assume that discrimination exists and be determined to eradicate it by constant attention to detail in practice and behaviour. Health authorities must take this seriously, whether or not they have large ethnic minority communities; gender discrimination has been common in some health services, e.g. cardiac surgery, in the past.

The government is also capable of discriminating unfairly, for example against mentally ill people. By tolerating abuse, domestic violence and insulting behaviour caused by alcohol but not tolerating any of these caused by (mental) illness, the government and society are discriminating against people with mental illness. This is apparent in the public relations attached to *Modernising Mental Health Services* and must not be repeated by health authorities who have a duty to meet the needs of patients.

Smoking kills

Central to the improvement of health overall, and especially to reducing inequalities in health between social groups, is a reduction in cigarette smoking. The government's long-promised, but delayed, White Paper on tobacco, *Smoking Kills* (a title of rare joy), proved disappointingly incomplete. While providing resources to support smoking cessation therapies and heralding a ban on tobacco advertising, there is no total ban on smoking in public places and the advertising ban is dependent on EU partners agreeing to the timescale and scope of the ban and may not be in place by 2006. In addition to specific targets (Box 3.13), there are proposed initiatives in promoting clean air, media campaigns against smoking, a drive against the smuggling of tobacco (and alcohol) products, research into quitting therapies, especially during pregnancy, and international action to raise duties overseas and develop joint action against tobacco.

Additional action is proposed to discourage young people from starting smoking and helping them to stop. Enforcement of the existing laws on under-age sales would help, as would the

---

Box 3.13   Targets for smoking reduction

- to halt the rise in children who smoke by reducing smoking among children from 13 to 11% by 2005 and to 9% by 2010

- to establish a new downward trend in adult smoking rates in all social classes by reducing smoking so that the overall rate falls from 28 to 26% by 2005 and to 24% or less by 2010

- to improve the health of expectant mothers and their families by reducing the percentage of women who smoke during pregnancy from 23 to 18% by 2005 and to 15% by 2010

mandatory use of proof-of-age cards. Limiting advertising and concealing vending machines may also help.

Most (70%) adults who smoke are dissonant (would like to give up) and the White Paper promises specific help with extra funding for initiating nicotine replacement therapy in people who live in HAZs. Priority will be given to helping pregnant women to give up smoking. Action plans must be developed by health authorities and PCGs as part of their HImPs.

The range and location of services

One of the core functions of health authorities is to determine the range and location of services, in hospitals and in the community. Central to the exercise of this function, in the shorter term, is the management of general hospital capacity to ensure the prompt

---

Box 3.14   Strategic initiatives in the range and location of services

- Reducing waiting times and waiting lists

- Whole systems initiatives to ensure ability of hospitals to deal with winter pressures

- Special commissioning arrangements for specialist health services

- NSFs for cancer, paediatric intensive care, heart disease and mental health

- *Better Services for Vulnerable People*

- National Priorities Guidance for health and social services

- *Information for Health*

- *Working Together*

- A national initiative on estates management, including a new approach to private and public sector investment in the NHS

- *Modernising Social Services*

- *Modernising Mental Health Services*

local management of emergencies and sufficient surgical service capacity to deliver political waiting list and waiting time targets. However, a growing list of other components of this strategy has emerged as the government progressively adds to the list of priorities (Box 3.14). Eventually, there is a risk that the government will fall victim, as did many of its predecessors, to priority fatigue – when everything is a priority, nothing is.

The comprehensive HImP will address not only NHS provision, but also independent sector healthcare, social services and related service provision, such as specialist housing (for the disabled, homeless and post-offending individuals). Key outputs include the development of services which cross traditional sectors to meet the complex needs of client groups; this may be assisted by legislation to permit the pooling of budgets (between health and local authorities) and more flexible transfer of funds between agencies. Another probable outcome will be the reconfiguration of services.

Reconfiguring NHS trusts

The configuration of NHS trusts inherited by the government was an unstructured network of community trusts, mental health trusts, learning disabilities trusts, acute hospitals trusts, combinations of any two, three or four of these and specialist trusts occupying part of a hospital. There were also specialist ambulance services trusts. Various mergers have taken place, mostly of like with like, and mixed trusts are being reconfigured along specialist or geographical lines. Vertical and horizontal integration is reducing the number of trusts but making little more sense than the original configuration. The proposals in the White Paper are starting to radically change the configuration of NHS trusts (Box 3.15).

Community health services will be transferred to Level 4 primary care trusts; mental health and learning disabilities services are increasingly being separated from acute general hospital services where they were combined and will be provided exclusively by specialist providers in order to sustain quality, develop specialisation and to reduce the risk of service failures leading to homicides; combined services trusts are therefore being reduced in size as they

---

Box 3.15   Triggering factors for NHS trust reconfiguration

- Transfer of community hospitals to primary care trusts (Level 4)

- Mental health and learning disabilities services to be managed by specialist providers

- Continued bearing down on NHS trust management costs

- Medical Royal College recommendations on the organisation of medical and surgical specialties for populations of 500 000

- The need to change the culture of NHS trusts to facilitate the new duty of partnership

- Tackling recurring deficits in NHS trusts

---

become restricted to general hospitals only and they will come under pressure to merge. As the pressure to reduce management costs continues to build, and community services are transferred to the new organisations, the number of NHS trusts remaining must reduce too in order to spread the management overheads. The medical Royal Colleges are making recommendations for the future organisation of hospital services that would operate on a much larger basis than the 250 000 population which was the guide for the development of the district general hospital. In future, general hospital services will be based on population catchments of at least 500 000 and the configuration of hospital trusts will follow.

The future configuration of providers will therefore be based on primary care trusts, specialist mental health/learning disabilities trusts and large general hospital trusts. Excluding primary care trusts, the total number of NHS trusts may fall from over 450 at the beginning of this parliament to about 200 by 2002.

More doctors but fewer beds

Larger hospital trusts will have much bigger teams of clinicians, perhaps working in more than one hospital and meeting Royal

College requirements for subspecialisation. Bigger teams with more specialists can develop tertiary service provision and the traditional district general hospital will cease to be universal. Future hospital models will include teaching hospitals, large general hospitals with some specialist services and small local hospitals offering a limited range of specialties.

The drive for greater efficiency in the hospital service will continue to put pressure on hospital bed numbers. Only the bigger hospitals will have the flexibility to survive.

The commissioning and provision of specialist services

Before the 1991 reforms, a wide range of specialist services, including dialysis, radiotherapy, transplantation, cardiac surgery, genetics services and neurosciences, were planned and funded by regional health authorities. In most cases, these responsibilities were transferred to district health authorities as part of the internal market. This has resulted in both fragmentation of the commissioning of services and complexity for their providers. Since 1996, health authorities have attempted to adopt collective approaches to the commissioning of these tertiary services to reduce their own financial risk (many of these services are rapidly growing and were structured as cost-per-case contracts with high unit costs) and the risk to the integrity of the services, often the most rapidly developing areas of hospital care, at the leading edge of technology, frequently emotive and often undergoing evaluation rather than of proven benefit. These moves, which are by no means universal, have generally been regarded as successful and the White Paper gives NHS Executive Regional Offices responsibility for ensuring that such arrangements are in place everywhere and operate effectively.

Precedents exist

Various supraregional service commissioning arrangements exist for services such as liver transplantation and complex cranio-facial surgery, which are provided by one provider for more than one region. The high-security psychiatric services commissioning board (for the special hospitals) and the national specialist commissioning advisory group fulfil these responsibilities and the services are funded through a national levy on all health authorities. These arrangements appear to work well in controlling costs, preventing creepage in service provision, maintaining the quality of services, and ensuring fair and equal access based only on clinical need, although there remains a tendency even for these services to be used preferentially by local residents. However, they represent only 10% of these highly specialised services by cost and regionally based services do not enjoy this systematic approach, access is unfair – heavily biased towards the populations situated close to the specialist providers – and there is a lack of specialist services commissioning expertise in health authorities.

The services and the funding

Following consultation on the proposals for specialist service commissioning in the White Paper, a revised list of services, based on agreed criteria (Box 3.16), to be covered in whole or in part (Box 3.17), was published in October 1998 together with national priorities (Box 3.18) to be taken forward during 1999. Such services, which tend to be small in volume and high in unit cost, can be funded through top-slicing, an equitable levy on the health authorities concerned, or through bottom-slicing, individual investment contributions offered by each authority, usually inequitably. The latter method, favoured by the internal market, does not result in equal access related to clinical need as health authorities face these services with different levels of affordability and variable positions among their own priorities. Many authorities favour their local providers and regard investment in specialist providers outside their own area as undesirable, although these services may offer excellent clinical value. As leading edge clinical services tend to be fast-growing, the tension between meeting justified clinical need and affordability can be very high. Some authorities tend to be isolationist and would rather commission these types of service from their own providers even though they may not possess the skills required; quality assurance is one of the principal aims of

---

Box 3.16   Criteria for selecting services for specialised commissioning

One or more of the following

- The planning population for the service is significantly greater than that of a single health authority (average size 500 000), because patient numbers are small and a critical mass is required at each centre to:
  - ensure optimum outcomes and sustain clinical competence
  - sustain training of specialised staff
  - support high-quality programmes of research
  - ensure cost-effectiveness of provision
  - ensure best use of scarce resources (expertise, equipment, donor organs)

- The service is in a fast-developing area, probably high-technology, where development and innovation need managing

- There are high-profile ethical issues (such as equity of access, high unit cost and small patient numbers) on which a region-wide approach is beneficial

---

collective commissioning and one of the first victims of fragmentation.

Each of the services identified as suitable for specialised commissioning exhibits one or more of the above criteria. Determining priorities from the long list will be decided on political issues or on collateral priority, such as a NSF.

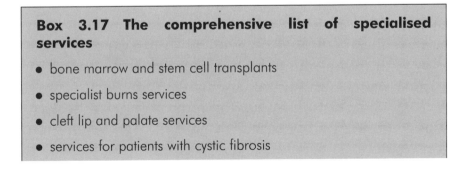

Box 3.17   The comprehensive list of specialised services

- bone marrow and stem cell transplants
- specialist burns services
- cleft lip and palate services
- services for patients with cystic fibrosis

- gender dysphoria (sex change), including mental health and surgical aspects
- clinical and laboratory genetics services
- haemophilia services
- specialised services for AIDS/HIV
- intestinal failure services
- neurosciences, including
  - clinical neurophysiology
  - complex multiple sclerosis and demyelinating disease
  - epilepsy with complex needs
  - interventional neuroradiology
  - neuropathology
  - neurosurgery
  - rare neurological diseases (e.g. myasthenia gravis)
  - specialised neurorehabilitation (e.g. after traumatic brain injury)
- renal replacement therapy (dialysis and transplantation)
- services for rare cancers
- specialised cardiology and cardiac surgery
  - heart and lung transplantation
  - cardiac electrophysiology
  - congenital heart disease in adults
- specialised maternity services
  - fetal medicine and prenatal diagnosis
  - management of high-risk pregnancies
  - tertiary infertility services
- specialised mental health services
  - assessment (and specialised treatment) for early dementia
  - eating disorder services
  - medium and high secure psychiatric services
  - services for people with sensory deficits (sight and/or hearing loss) and severe mental illness
  - mother and baby psychiatric units

- specialist psychotherapies
- specialist services for people with personality disorder

- specialised pathology services
  - immunological pathology
  - transplantation-associated and other specialist pathology for renal and hepatic disease
  - other specialist clinical pathology (e.g. bone tumour pathology)

- specialised services for addictions

- specialised services for infectious diseases (e.g. drug-resistant tuberculosis, viral haemorrhagic fevers)

- specialised services for people with learning disabilities
  - forensic services for people with learning disabilities and very challenging behaviour and other complex needs
  - services for autism and Asperger's syndrome

- specialised services for people with physical disabilities and chronic illness
  - communication aids (e.g. bone-anchored hearing aids)
  - complex orthotics and prosthetics (seating, special artificial limbs and appendages)
  - environmental controls
  - high-technology home aids
  - inpatient complex assessment and rehabilitation
  - specialised wheelchair provision

- spinal injuries services

- tertiary services for children
  - cardiology
  - gastroenterology
  - oncology
  - specialised child and adolescent mental health services
  - metabolic disorders
  - neonatal intensive care
  - paediatric intensive care
  - endocrinology

> - immunological disorders and infectious diseases, including AIDS
> - rheumatology
> - paediatric pathology
> - neonatal and infant cardiac surgery
> - neurosciences and neuropsychiatry
>
> ● screening services (being handled through a separate mechanism)

Many of these specialist services were added to the list as a result of the consultation conducted by the government during the spring and summer of 1998. It represents a desire by the government to avoid any form of conflict with the professions based on judgement of relative priorities, therefore, if the professions want them in the list, in the list they will be. In practice, however, the list is so long that only work on government-selected services will be taken forward.

> **Box 3.18 National priorities for specialist service commissioning in 1999/2000**
>
> ● Medium and high secure psychiatric services (in conjunction with the shadow devolution of the functions of the High Security Psychiatric Services Commissioning Team – expected to be abolished in 2000 or 2001)
>
> ● Services for patients with cleft lip and palate – following guidance published by the Clinical Standards Advisory Group in 1997
>
> ● Other specialised services described in the NSFs for coronary heart disease and mental health (published during 1999)

NHS Executive Regional Offices were required to establish organisational arrangements to facilitate this work. In those regions where collective health authority mechanisms had been introduced, these tended to be rubber stamped, reviewed early in 1999 and overall work programmes considered for the full list of services. In practice, this usually involved giving priority to those services already subject to joint authority commissioning and identifying lead responsibility for the others – just in case.

Partnership again

The population base for these services is over one million, sometimes many more. This is larger than almost all health authorities and therefore requires multiauthority approaches. As the only expert knowledge about these services resides in the providers themselves, they too need to be involved in the planning process. Only in this way can the confidence of providers, especially the clinicians, in the process be assured. The services involved are not only among the fastest-growing health services, they are of potentially very high added value. They are best developed, supported and utilised effectively through top-sliced funding arrangements. As these reforms are implemented, the restructuring of health authorities and the redrawing of their boundaries may well be based on the catchment areas for these highly specialised services to integrate their commissioning at the level of the populations served. However, the existing commissioning expertise will not be based in health authorities in the future; they will be strategic organisations and PCGs will employ the commissioning staff, on whose behalf these specialised services are commissioned. Specialist providers will recoil in horror at the prospect of having to deal with up to 25 PCGs; their experience with fundholders, not necessarily representative of the future, will have shown them that small commissioners think small; these services require vision and overview. The development of specialist commissioning units for these services, at Regional Office, multiauthority or individual authority level is possible, but in all cases the providers must be involved. A more rational model would be to integrate the commissioning and the provision of some of these services, such as specialised mental health services, with a regional commissioning board representing health authorities and PCGs to oversee balance and affordability. This would be an example of true vertical integration within a specialist NHS trust.

National Service Frameworks

The cancer model

Amidst the growing chaos of the NHS internal market, the Chief Medical Officers of England and Wales (Kenneth Calman and Dierdre Hine) attempted something unusually bold in the midst of John Major's Conservative administration; they published a model centralist plan for cancer services which was so good that even the then government had to accept it. The eponymous authors had left little to chance, securing professional support and arranging for publication of their report without informing the NHS Executive. The health service found various ways of implementing the report and found that it liked planning and that health services benefited as a result. Thanks to the Calman–Hine report, the NHS has redis-covered the joys of planning, the relationships it forges, the horizontal and vertical integration, the unifying goals of better healthcare for both managers and clinicians, etc. The proposed NSFs are based on the Calman–Hine approach, which uses evidence-based approaches to complex planning issues and enables rational planning for services to patients which cross many sectors of care and several tiers of services. The proposed services to be handled in this way will include coronary heart disease (1999), mental health for adults (1999), services for older people (including mental health) – jointly with social services (2000), health and social services for children (including mental health) in 2001 and diabetes (2001); the approach will encourage a patient-focused model of services leading to commissioned programmes of care. A conti-nuing programme of frameworks will develop during the next ten years, covering an increasing proportion of the total spectrum of healthcare.

Rolling out the genre

The arrangements for establishing the new frameworks were announced with some panoply in the days before the fiftieth anniversary of the NHS, in late June 1998. The announcement stated that NSFs would specify the type of services that should be available in all primary care, local hospitals and specialist centres. They would also set down tough quality standards that would have to be met across the NHS. The brief for mental health focuses on adults of working age, although the complex needs of those at the end of adolescence and the beginning of older age are also addressed. (Mental health in older people will be covered by the NSF for older people due in 2000 and for children and adolescents in 2001.) The brief for coronary heart disease focuses on partnership working by the NHS and local authorities, with an emphasis on health promotion and disease prevention.

External reference groups were appointed for each framework, chaired by leading academics (George Alberti for coronary heart disease and Graham Thornicroft for mental health), and charged with publishing their emerging findings within three months and their final reports within nine months – targets almost met by the heart group but effectively abandoned by the mental health group. Terms of reference were published (Box 3.19) and further investment in heart disease research was announced.

The reference groups adopted an inclusive approach, engaging a full range of views through an open website and a number of subgroups, each dealing with a chapter of the final report. The groups were especially interested in examples of effective local partnerships. These, together with research reviews, underpin the basis of service standards and models.

The performance of the groups themselves proved highly variable. For heart disease, things apparently went swimmingly, building on a sound platform of national standards and significant

Box 3.19 Terms of reference for external reference groups for the National Service Frameworks 1999

To present proposals to ministers for a National Service Framework which will set national standards and define service models for coronary heart disease/mental health; put in place strategies to support implementation; and establish performance measures against which progress within an agreed timescale will be measured

success already in improving services and outcomes. In mental health, however, major philosophical problems emerged between the medical academics, who saw things in strictly clinical terms, and the other professionals and service user representatives, who tended to take a much broader view of mental illness and the means of responding to it. It has even been suggested that the tension between the chairman, who was seen by some as representing the psychiatric establishment, and the DoH's officers led to threats of resignation (by the chairman). Intervention by Frank Dobson prevented such a disastrous outcome but the differences persisted right up to the point of the final report being redrafted by officials. Emerging findings, promised in September/October, did not emerge and some preliminary ideas on values, principles and structural service elements were written by officials as part of the mental health strategy, *Modernising Mental Health Services*. Furthermore, an unfortunate statement by a new minister (Hutton) had led to the representatives of service users walking out of the External Reference Group. A brave face was put on all of this by all concerned and, in the end, it probably made little difference to the outcome.

One consequence of these experiences was the early announcement of the frameworks for older people, children and for diabetes, and the establishment of the necessary groups, infrastructure and more generous timescales.

NSFs constitute an important part of the national strategy for quality in healthcare. They are designed to ensure that uniformly high standards of care are available to all patients, wherever they are and whoever provides the service. They contribute to the elimination of inappropriate variations in patient care; they provide for managers and planners what the NICE will do for clinicians; the progress in implementing the frameworks will be the subject of reviews by the CHI. They will eventually be constructed in a standard format with ease of reference for monitoring and with three specific components (Box 3.20). Intermediate milestones will be set which will be monitored locally via NHS Executive Regional Offices, later by the regular reviews by the CHI. The selection of areas suitable for developing a NSF will be closely linked to other government initiatives, including their priorities for overall health improvement described in the National Priorities Guidance – as it

> **Box 3.20   Key components of National Service Frameworks**
>
> - setting **national standards** and defining **service models** for a specific service or care group
>
> - putting in place programmes to support **implementation**
>
> - establishing **performance indicators** against which progress within an agreed timescale will be measured

is revised over time – and the national priorities covered by the *Saving Lives: Our Healthier Nation* White Paper and subsequent developments in public health action.

The most difficult of these assignments may well be the performance indicators, given the ineptitude of NHS measurement in the past. Determining indicators of performance which actually make a difference to patients, as opposed to providing material for minister's speeches, is indeed a challenge.

The schedule for the implementation of NSFs is to commence planning in the year of their publication with commencement of implementation through the HImP for the following year. So, for the frameworks for coronary heart disease and mental health, the HImP for 1999/2000 includes outline plans for implementation based on the emerging findings and specific plans for service development, including milestones and performance criteria, will form part of the HImP for 2000/03.

Modernising Mental Health Services

The government's strategy for mental health services was published in December 1998. It describes itself as providing for mental health services which are safe, sound and supportive: safe in terms of reducing risk to the public from mentally ill people; sound in terms of ensuring a full range of local services; supportive for service users and staff. The strategy was accompanied by a publicity campaign, which clearly implied that mentally ill people constituted a risk to public safety and had to be controlled, an approach which succeeded in pandering to the nastier elements of the British media and which managed to alienate almost everyone involved in mental health services, including service users of course.

Thus, the government has handled the complex forces for change in mental health services by a paradoxical dual approach to its strategy: combining an accusation that community care has failed with a service strategy which is clearly founded on community care principles. To avoid the service failures which have afflicted public perceptions of mental health services for so long, the strands of the strategy are to develop inclusive and accessible services which are modern, comprehensive and evidence-based and integrated with all other agencies providing services for mentally ill people. The

---

Box 3.21   Priorities for implementing modern mental health services

- strengthening comprehensive care by filling gaps in services such as
  - acute psychiatric hospital beds
  - 24-hour nursed care
  - secure psychiatric beds
  - assertive outreach teams
  - crisis intervention services

- providing 24-hour access to services

- developing, training and recruiting staff

- improving the planning and commissioning of mental health services

- developing partnership working
  - at strategic level, throughout the NHS and across agencies
  - at operational level, integrating care programme approach and case management
  - at interpersonal level, involving users and carers more in care decisions and processes

- improving the use of IT

- developing mental health promotion

priority areas for development are shown in Box 3.21. The fundamental issue is comprehensiveness; many other strategies have been tried and have failed, at least in part, but they all lacked the background of comprehensive service support.

A new legal framework is clearly required in mental health, the existing Act being based on a different age and too limited in terms of its scope. The government is reviewing the current Mental Health Act and the need for reform but it may not be easy to find parliamentary time in the foreseeable future.

There is significant disquiet with the government's attitude on mental health. Successive ministers have alienated staff and service users and the continuing obsession with the risks posed by people with mental illness is stifling debate on the real issues: how to improve the effectiveness of treatment and how to improve the sensitivity of services. The government is committed to joining up both policy and operational services and appears to be making substantial resources available, although closer analysis shows much of this to be an illusion (see Box 3.29). Such an approach makes controversy inevitable. It is important, for those who advocate user involvement in services, that the negative public presentation of the government's intentions does not distract from the considerable opportunity which the strategy offers. It demands leadership, vision and commitment; what a shame that the government does not provide these itself.

Information for Health

The NHS boasts a long and undistinguished history of failed investment in information technology. The underlying problem, apart from a lack of competitive expertise, is that the NHS has computerised its archaic systems rather than using technology to revolutionise its systems and processes. While the rest of the world speeds up and shrinks through the use of miniature, satellite-linked communication tools, the NHS grinds its pedestrian way towards the millennium with old mainframes, manual systems and slow communications. The technology required to deliver the revolution has been in existence for 20 years and in widespread use for more than a decade in other industries. In the *Information Strategy for the*

Box 3.22   Specific seven-year objectives of *Information for Health*

- reliable and rapid access to relevant personal information, 24 hours a day, to support professionals providing patient care

- eliminate unnecessary travel and delay through the use of on-line access to services, specialists and care

- to provide accredited, independent, multimedia information and advice to NHS patients about their condition

- to provide on-line access to local guidance and national evidence on treatment for NHS professionals, and the information they need to evaluate their work

- make available accurate information for managers and planners to support HImPs and the National Framework for Assessing Performance

- provide fast and convenient access for the public to accredited multimedia advice on lifestyle and health, and information to support public involvement in local and national policy development

Modern NHS 1998–2005, Frank Burns has applied the existing technologies to a plan to radically change the culture of healthcare, backed by promises of substantial additional funding from the government, starting with the Modernisation Fund.

During the seven years of the strategy, the government intends to achieve six specific objectives (Box 3.22). At the heart of the initiative is the vision of seamless care facilitated by creating an Electronic Health Record (EHR), a lifelong and transferable record containing all core clinical information. Within the hospital setting, Electronic Patient Records (EPRs) will support organisational requirements while enabling information exchange.

The overall cost of the new investment required is estimated to be £1 billion over the seven years. Of this sum, £70 million was available in the first year, mostly to improve resources in primary care (*see* Box 3.29). However, the real cost could well be much higher and the real benefits are substantially in cultural change

> **Box 3.23   Preparing for implementation of *Information for Health***
>
> - connect all computerised GP practices to the NHSnet (an intranet with appropriate confidentiality and security systems for personal healthcare – the NHS superhighway) by the end of 1999 to enable electronic data interchange about hospital appointments and test results
>
> - enabling everyone in England to contact NHS Direct (the 24-hour nurse-led, telephone advice line) by the end of 2000
>
> - setting up 'beacon' sites to pioneer and develop EHRs
>
> - ensuring health authorities, NHS trusts and PCGs have the right support at both national and regional level to buy the best services and systems and avoid unnecessary duplication

rather than in direct benefits. Traditionally, managers' eyes have glazed over at the first mention of information; it will take more than publishing a strategy and exhorting the NHS to do better to create the excitement this strategy deserves. Lead responsibility for implementing the strategy falls to health authorities, who, it has to be acknowledged, have no history and few skills in this field.

The initial steps for implementation, overseen by the NHS Executive, are shown in Box 3.23. Joint work between the NHS and local authorities, and specific investment in the development of health informatics services in 2000/01 are also features of the implementation plan.

Working Together

The NHS workforce strategy was launched with a whimper, has political support but without passion and has little in the manner of tangible assets to back it up. Entitled *Working Together – securing a quality workforce for the NHS*, it was released during the late summer of 1998, close to *Information for Health*, which enjoyed all the tangible and ministerial commitment that *Working Together*

Box 3.24   The strategic aims of *Working Together*

1 The NHS must ensure that it has a quality workforce, in the right numbers, with the right skills and diversity, organised in the right way, to deliver the government's service objectives for health and social care.

2 It must be able to demonstrate it is improving the quality of working life for staff

3 It must address the management capacity and capability required to deliver this agenda and the associated programme of change

---

Box 3.25   Short-term (by April 2000) targets for employers

• Record, monitor and publish a strategy to reduce workplace accidents and violence against staff

• Institute policies and procedures to tackle harassment by staff and service users

• Make available occupational health and counselling services for all staff

• The majority of health professionals to have training and development plans

• Develop mechanisms for involving staff in planning and delivering healthcare

• Reduce sickness absence rates towards national minimum bench marks

• Improve retention rates for all health professions

• Undertake an annual staff attitude survey to measure improvements in quality of working life

lacked. The three strategic aims (Box 3.24) are supported by short-term targets (Box 3.25) and an implementation plan.

National action is required to establish underpinning values, to sort out the mess over pay which results from the experiments with local pay determination, to clarify the educational framework for the health professions and to institute long-term workforce planning. Experience with the medical profession, which has enjoyed central control of workforce numbers for over 40 years, suggests that success will be elusive, medicine having lurched from one miscalculation to another. The absence of geographical barriers to workforce movement, at least within the EU, renders any nation-based calculations tentative at best.

Enormous investment is being made to shore up the nursing profession, hit by a crisis largely of its own making. Nursing, as a profession, lacks any uniqueness; it is basically a combination of all the things that nurses do. The scope of activities covered by nursing has extended in recent years, partly to cover ground left behind by doctors as their working curve shifts towards the more technical and partly to reflect the growth of specialist work created by nurses themselves. The result is that nursing covers a huge range of work and there is no single strategy that can solve its problems. Investing huge sums in recruitment and retention is of questionable value if the purpose of nurses is unclear. The confusion of leadership in the profession is a major obstacle; is the Royal College of Nursing primarily a trade union or a professional organisation? The United Kingdom Central Council for Nursing, Midwifery and Health Visiting (UKCC) cannot lead the profession as it is its regulator. The post of Chief Nursing Officer has gradually been eroded in authority and few nurses could answer the question 'who leads the nursing profession?' The government has introduced a number of gimmicks such as nurse consultants and discretionary points for nurses, apeing medicine, but they are of no relevance to the vast majority of nurses or to the performance of the NHS.

Modernising Social Services

The social services White Paper, promised in April 1998, did not appear until the end of the year. By this time, early fears among social services staff that they were about to be taken over by the NHS had been greatly reduced by inaction and clear indications from ministers that major reconfiguration of public services was not in their minds. *Modernising Social Services* is a complementary paper to *The New NHS*, using similar language and principles. Underlying concerns are similar to those in the NHS: ineffective care at the interface with health, inflexible services which fail to meet individual's needs, weak safeguards for the vulnerable, a lack of clear standards of service the public can expect, inconsistency of service availability and charging, and inefficiency.

The White Paper closely reflects the National Priorities Guidance, with a specific focus on improving services for vulnerable children and adults, but also sets out actions to improve the quality of services (Box 3.26).

New resources are promised for social services, forming part of the ubiquitous Modernisation Fund. As with the NHS, however, the funds partly replace existing allocations rather than offering new net resources. A partnership grant (£650 million over three years) will

---

Box 3.26 The main proposals in *Modernising Social Services*

- establishing eight independent regional commissions for care standards to take over regulatory functions of local and health authorities for residential and nursing homes and to extend cover to other services such as care agencies

- better support for adults requiring care and support, including offering direct payments to older people to spend on care of their own design and choice

- appointing children's rights officers to provide more support and protection to vulnerable children

- establishing a new General Social Care Council to improve the regulation and training of social work staff

- introducing a Modernisation Fund for social services, providing £1.3 billion over three years to support implementation of the White Paper

foster partnership between health and social services to promote independence for adults, including avoidance of hospital admissions and earlier discharge. The spending plans will be stated in Joint Investment Plans. In addition, £100 million is available in a prevention grant to help support people most at risk of losing their independence; these plans also to be drawn up jointly with the NHS.

To ensure that adequate action is taken in response to the White Paper on looked-after children, *Quality Protects*, a children's services grant of £375 million will be targeted at specific action plans in each local authority. Legislation will be passed to extend the period of local authority responsibility from age 16 to 18. Overall, including general increases in assessments of need for local authority funding for social services, expenditure during the period 1999–2002 will rise by £3 billion, although this triple counts early growth and assumes that councils spend their allocation as the formula intends – unlike the NHS, they are under no obligation to do so except for the Modernisation Fund.

The White Paper introduces the proposed framework for the assessment of performance in social services as part of an extensive set of plans for improving the efficiency and quality of services. As with the NHS, these measures are based on comparisons between authorities rather than absolute values of best practice; the improvements in efficiency will be gained by all authorities attaining the level of the best.

The medium-term financial strategy

The comprehensive spending review

The comprehensive spending review (CSR) was initiated to enable the government to increase spending in its key areas, health and education, without increasing visible taxes. By diverting planned growth from less politically popular (or watched) areas to these priorities, and also by redefining the baseline in some cases, the government was able to claim, on publication of its White Paper *Modern Public Services: investing for reform* that real terms (after adjusting for inflation) spending on health would grow by 4.7% per annum between 1999 and 2002. In addition, annual real terms growth of 3.1% per annum was promised for social services. By adding together the cumulative annual additions in funding, the government was able to claim that the NHS was receiving an additional £17 654 million whereas, in fact, the spending in the third year compared with the baseline will be increased by only £8672 million. These increases assumed inflation rates much lower than was realistic (pay inflation in 1999/2000 was over 4% compared with a budgeted assumption of 2.5%) and included a much higher than average increase in capital expenditure (about 60%), mainly for information technology and various national initiatives such as A&E departments. In addition, a large proportion of the real growth, both capital and revenue, has been retained by the DoH in the form of the £5 billion Modernisation Fund which is being used by ministers to ensure that their promises, such as reducing waiting lists, are properly funded, even if it means no resources for local discretion.

A further confounding factor in the hope raised by the announcement of the CSR was the very high level of efficiency gains expected from services throughout the period. Both health and social services are expected to release 3% each year through greater efficiency. While services are used to generating efficiency in the form of reduced unit costs through raising activity within a fixed budget, it increasingly appears that the 3% is expected to be released in the equivalent of cash. This is almost certainly more than services can realistically deliver and is heading services towards financial disaster.

The Chancellor had announced that the new money was only available for delivering services and that the Modernisation Fund was only to be used for changing standards. In the event, the Fund was raided even before the period in question had begun in order to pay for part of the nurses' pay award in 1999. In effect, 6% of the total fund was committed to this cause from the outset.

The resources

The actual funding available to the NHS in the year before the CSR and for the three years covered by the review are shown in Box 3.27.

Box 3.27   Key figures for the NHS in the comprehensive spending review

	1998/99 (pre-CSR)	1999/2000	2000/01	2001/02
NHS total	£36 507m	£39 581m	£42 415m	£45 179m
real growth		5.7%	4.5%	3.9%
NHS current	£36 279m	£39 301m	£42 062m	£44 768m
NHS capital	£228m	£280m	£352m	£411m

The Modernisation Fund is subsequently deducted from these figures, both capital and revenue. The proposed approach was for the government to inform public services of three years' funding well in advance so that they could plan services in the medium term. In the event, this was not done in time for the 1999/2000 HImPs and may not be done at all, although social services had a clearer indication of their prospects than the NHS. It appeared as if the amount and use of the Modernisation Fund was being invented as events unfolded. It was also increasingly clear that the government was intent on retrospectively counting existing expenditure as part of the Fund. For example, see Box 3.28 on how the

Box 3.28   Breakdown of mental health modernisation funds 1999/2000

Total Modernisation Fund for mental health 1999/2000   £146m

- Adult mental health services   £40m
  of which £19m included in HA baseline allocations to fund:
  - 220 additional 24-hour staffed places
  - 13 assertive outreach teams
  - improved access to services throughout 24 hours
  - cost of new prescribing of atypical antipsychotic drugs
  - £21m available to be bid for to meet rising demand for medium secure beds and for training

- Child and adolescent mental health services – biddable   £10m

- Strategic Assistance Fund for Mentally Disordered Offenders forming part of HA baseline allocations but actually allocated in 1997 as challenge funding   £15m

- Mental Health Partnership Fund forming part of HA baseline allocations but allocated during 1998 as biddable funds   £4m

- Mental Health Promotion – centrally held fund   £1m

- Support for education and training for doctors and nurses but already levied via MADEL/NMET   £12m

- Estimated expenditure on drug treatments already allocated to HAs without definition   £17m

- Mental Health Grant to adult social services   £38m

- Child and adolescent mental health services – social services bids   £8m

so-called Modernisation Fund for mental health shapes up in 1999/2000.

Somewhat perversely, the CSR may well actually result in a tighter financial future for the NHS than it has experienced for several years. The inability of the government to fulfil its promise to give three-year funding allocations to health authorities has rendered the whole exercise fairly pointless as has the pre-emption of the Modernisation Fund by inflationary pay awards for staff. Indeed, with so much of the fund pre-empted by government gimmicks, unplanned initiatives and retro-rationalisation of existing expenditure, the existence of the Fund and the centralisation which goes with it will make medium-term planning harder than ever. For the first year (1999/2000), almost £560 million was retained by the government (Box 3.29), while almost as much was retro-fitted to resources already allocated to health authorities.

Finance and the HImP

It is vital that the planning of expenditure fits intimately with the planning of services. The coordination of services across sectors

Box 3.29   1999/2000 Health Modernisation Fund centrally retained funds

1 Waiting list bonus and booked admissions initiative	£50m
2 Reducing cancer outpatient waiting times	£10m
3 Closing down GP fundholding	£19m
4 Other primary care (and beacon practice) initiatives	£5m
5 Information technology for PCGs	£20m
6 Primary care infrastructure	£3m
7 Preparatory costs for Primary Care Act pilots	£1m
8 General practice out-of-hours cover	£2m
9 Paediatric intensive care beds	£5m
10 Services for lung cancer	£10m
11 Health Action Zones	£49m
12 Adult mental health (secure beds, training, 24-hour staffed beds, etc.)	£22m
13 Child and adolescent mental health	£10m
14 National screening pilots (for colorectal cancer)	£3m
15 Commission for Health Improvement	£3m
16 Diana nurses (child health in the community)	£1.4m
17 NHS Direct roll-out	£44m
18 National Institute for Clinical Excellence	£10m
19 Nurse prescribing	£5m
20 Staff training (via the NMET levy)	£10m
21 Staff pay – contribution to excess cost of 1999/2000 Review Body Award	£100m
22 National Patient Survey	£2m
23 Public health (central services, smoking action) (subsequently reduced to £25m through delay in publishing White Paper)	£45m
24 Capital (waiting lists, A&E, pathology, NSFs)	£70m
25 Information technology	£50m

also requires a coordination of financial planning between especially health and social services. The HImP therefore has to increasingly recognise the financial position of key partners as well as using the opportunity of the integrated budget to think flexibly about the distribution of resources within the NHS.

The National Framework for Assessing Performance

The main parameters of the assessment of performance have been described in Part 2 of this book and the key elements listed in Boxes 2.17 and 2.18. As the framework matures, more in terms of experience than detail, its influence on the management of change in the NHS will emerge with increasing strength. The use of measurement in an increasing range of parameters of NHS practice stimulates observers, and especially the government, to identify variations with a view to reducing them. The White Paper, and the government's expectations in terms of efficiency savings, require exemplary performance of all providers in order to reduce both variations and costs.

For the purposes of the HImP, health authorities are the owners of the data that determine which variations justify action. Initial priorities, because they require only a single measurement rather than a trend, will include fair access to services and relative efficiency of hospital services. Longer-term work will focus on health improvement and the effective delivery of appropriate care. The key culture change relies on a focus on the other two dimensions of performance, the health outcomes of NHS care and the patient/carer experience of the NHS.

Health authorities will increasingly use comparisons and trends in these key performance indicators to set the agenda for better management of resources and increased clinical and service performance. The HImP is the mechanism by which these observations are converted into coordinated action to deliver better healthcare at lower cost to more people in an equitable way.

The framework remains excessively focused on acute general hospital activity with relatively weak measurement of primary and community-based services and clinical effectiveness. Further development in these areas is required and local experimentation by health authorities can be used to promote ideas. HAZs are especially likely to feature here, especially regarding joint analysis of community-based services in partnership with social services and creating harmony between the National Framework for Assessing Performance (NFAP) for the NHS and the equivalent framework for social care.

Involving service users and the public

It is not intended that HImPs will be traditional NHS planning documents, written in an attic, circulated for comment (consultation) and then published unabridged. For the HImP, patient and public involvement is meant to be effective throughout, in such a way that formal public consultation is not really necessary. The principal thrust of the government's strategy on patient and public empowerment has been through information. In general terms, information is power; hierarchies – including structural hierarchies between tiers of management and knowledge hierarchies between professionals and clients – are based on power through the acquisition and retention of information. Features such as NHS Direct, promotion of the use of the Internet and the dissemination of the evidence on effective healthcare direct to the public, presentation of HImPs in a form suitable for public engagement, etc., are signals of the overall shift in power through information which is envisaged.

Health authorities need to take their responsibilities in this regard very seriously. This is an aspect of public confidence where the NHS has a very poor record, where management has mimicked professional colleagues in dismissing the public as, at best, semi-educated and half-informed meddlers. In the post-Thatcher/Major Britain, however, dismissal of the people as periodic voting fodder who exercise their vote in a purely selfish way is no longer a valid response. Encouraged by the Blair government, the public increasingly expects to be taken seriously and to be consulted as well as informed.

The requirement is for a new mind-set among NHS agencies in

which the public, and their patients in particular, are treated as equal stakeholders in all service issues, including the shaping and planning of services and the monitoring of their performance. In local government, these principles are embraced by Best Value. In the NHS, no equivalent structure exists but its philosophy needs to be created if the culture change required by the NHS is to become a reality.

Be in no doubt that these changes will happen in time. The British people have endured suboptimal services in an unfriendly style for too long; the worm will turn and this government is the first to genuinely attempt to stimulate it. However, the outcome is likely to be rapidly rising expectations which neither the service providers nor HM Treasury is equipped to meet.

The shape of Health Improvement Programmes' accountability and monitoring

The HImP will be a long and complex programme, covering an increasing list of government priorities, embracing the strategic drivers described above and encompassing the range of actions to improve health described in *Saving Lives: Our Healthier Nation*. Developing the programme will become an increasingly industrious process and ensuring its implementation will become the most arduous task. This task, like most of the others involved in the work programme of the HImP, falls to health authorities.

The primary responsibility of the health authority is to provide the strategic vision and commitment which makes possible the culture change whose achievement is the ultimate goal of the new NHS. It is within this vision that the exercise of its role of coordination and ensuring the delivery of the NHS agencies' responsibilities for implementation takes root.

As the individual programmes evolve, especially the complex multiagency programmes such as that for older people, attributing responsibilities to participating organisations becomes a major component of the implementation plan. It is clear that the ambitions of such programmes require the commitment and engagement of organisations which have no direct relationship to the NHS. This particularly applies to the smaller local authorities in Shire counties and to the previously less engaged partners, such as police, probation and fire services, in terms of achieving targets to reduce accidents and to tackle drug misuse.

Within the NHS family, both NHS trusts and PCGs/trusts must recognise and accept their responsibilities to deliver their commitments as part of the HImP and to acknowledge the primacy of the health authority. This may come hard to some NHS trusts but the greater difficulty could well be encountered with PCGs. Many GPs have a strangely dismissive attitude towards health authorities, founded on their limited exposure to their work in commissioning compared with the cut and thrust of fundholding. However, if PCGs take their responsibilities seriously, they will soon come to see the health authorities as their rock rather than their swamp. A further complication is that many of the new responsibilities of health authorities, such as workforce planning and information technology, lie outwith their recent experience and current expertise. In the foreseeable future, many existing health authority responsibilities will transfer to primary care trusts and the power base of health authorities will rest largely with the HImP and the coordination and orchestration of the community of stakeholders. It is highly likely, though not yet admitted, that health authorities will only be able to fulfil this role if the other NHS bodies are directly accountable to them. At present, guidance to this effect applies to primary care trusts but not to NHS trusts, except in respect of their responsibilities in respect of implementing the HImP. No doubt there will be further reorganisations of these structures before the new organisations have time to become fully mature; this is the seventh major restructuring of the NHS since 1974. It is not even certain that the format and philosophy of the current HImP will endure, although something similar will be required whatever else happens. The overriding principles of partnership and collective responsibility constitute the essence of public services for the next generation.

Part 4

Quality in the new NHS

Introduction

The government's commitment to improving the quality of health-care, in terms of both outcome and the experience of receiving care, has been clear and consistent since its election. Their motives comprise the usual mixture of altruism – doing the best for the people – and self-interest in that an excellent NHS reflects well on the government. This latter point is probably a vain hope as all the good in healthcare is regarded by the public as being attributable to doctors and nurses, while all that is bad is the fault of managers and their political masters. Nonetheless, the framework for quality described in the White Paper and, in more detail, in *A First Class Service*, has many strengths and few detractors.

Overall, the framework is elegant and simple. The NICE will commission, approve and disseminate evidence-based guidelines for clinical practice; NSFs will provide a secure and evidence-based structure for the development of service organisation and delivery for managers to plan for. The process known as clinical governance will ensure that the professions deliver the service recommended by the NICE guidelines, with the promise/threat of stronger profes-sional self-regulation and a strategy of lifelong education to back it up. Similarly, the HImP process is the means by which health authorities, NHS trusts and PCGs must implement the NSFs. Just in case these mechanisms are not sufficient on their own, supporting evidence of effectiveness will come from the NFAP (of the whole NHS) and the patient and user survey will provide a customer's view of the performance of the local and national NHS. To police the system, a new organisation, the CHI, will come along and make serious trouble for any organisation or group of professionals who have not done as they were told.

So far, so good. All that stands in the way of a glorious triumph is the lack of reliable evidence, the people to do the job and human nature. Most surprising of all perhaps, in an era when money is being thrown at politically important initiatives such as the manifesto commitment to reduce waiting lists, is that absolutely no funding is made available to support the implementation of the quality strategy.

The underlying philosophy, as we have seen before, is that variations in practice are too wide to be justifiable and, that if a clear

---

Box 4.1 Concerns driving the quality agenda

- The NHS does not match modern expectations of rapid access to high-quality services

- Well-publicised lapses in quality have prompted doubts about the overall standards of care people receive

- It is not good enough for excellent care to be available for some patients but not for others

- There are unacceptable variations in performance and practice

- Proven treatments are introduced too slowly while unproven treatments are introduced too quickly

- Inequalities in waiting times, in the number receiving screening, in clinical practice and outcomes

- Concern at the number of patients being denied proven treatment by delay in professionals and managers acting on published evidence

way of doing things is agreed, no variation from that norm is acceptable.

A wide range of public and political concerns underpin the comprehensive strategy for quality in the new NHS (Box 4.1). These concerns have gradually emerged during the past decade, driven partly by previous structural change and partly by the public and media obsession with health, healthcare and the attribution of blame for anything that can go wrong.

Eliminating variations

Variations in practice are held to explain variations in outcome (Box 4.2). The professions are not generally held responsible; more they are regarded as victims of a system which these proposals set out to change. However, unjustified variations in care are wasteful and unfair.

By setting clear national standards (NICE and NSFs), local arrangements to ensure consistent and dependable delivery of services (clinical governance supported by lifelong learning and professional self-regulation) and having robust monitoring of standards (CHI, NFAP and the patient and user survey), the government intends to eradicate unjustified variations in practice, removing the so-called postcode medicine (different policies depending on where people lived) and raising standards of practice overall. This is all very well, but the government's language does

---

Box 4.2 The complex causes of variations in quality

- The NHS internal market shattered the national unity of the NHS and created perverse disincentives to sharing best practice

- Even before the internal market, there were no national standards of care which all were expected to achieve

- There has never been any coherent assessment of which treatments work best for which patients

- The NHS, as a public service, has not been sufficiently open and accountable for the quality of service it offers to the public

---

Box 4.3 Worrying language

'There will be a new emphasis on quality at all levels in the NHS. One that no longer tolerates failure but celebrates success'

---

cause some concern for the professions (Box 4.3). This implies that, in a service provided by a million staff for 60 million people, universal success can be guaranteed; this will never be the case.

Setting standards

The quality initiative is enabled by the growing success of the NHS R&D strategy, which has provided access to a rapidly expanding evidence base on healthcare interventions and services. The translation of this knowledge into guidance for professionals and managers has been confusing and inefficient. This will be remedied by the establishment of NICE and a programme of NSFs (Box 4.4) and for public health and health promotion by the Health Development Agency (Appendix 2).

The clear quality standards emerging from these mechanisms will be expected to be met by the whole of the NHS. This will prove extremely challenging to individual clinicians and to general practices; it could also lead to huge rises in costs as the concealed rationing of the past decade or more becomes exposed by guidelines based on the evidence alone. The chairman of NICE, Sir Michael Rawlins, has already made it clear that he will state things

---

Box 4.4 The new national standard-setting agencies

- The new NICE will promote clinical and cost-effectiveness, through guidance and audit, to support frontline staff. It will advise on best practice in the use of existing treatments, appraise new treatments, and advise the NHS on how they can be implemented and how best they fit alongside existing treatments

- Evidence-based NSFs will set out what patients can expect to receive from the NHS in major care areas or disease groups

the way he sees them, regardless of the sensitivities and without regard to affordability per se. As a robust chairman of the Committee on the Safety of Medicines for many years, Rawlins's stance ensures that the government will recognise the potential risks very seriously.

The six stages of standard setting

The work of NICE is only a small part of the whole process of generating and setting standards and monitoring them. *A First Class Service* describes the six stages of achieving consistent clinical standards across the NHS (Box 4.5).

A new partnership, the Horizon Scanning Centre, has been set up at the University of Birmingham in partnership with the National Prescribing Centre and the Drug Information Pharmacists Group, to fulfil the requirements of Stage 1. The second stage is the responsibility of the NHS R&D programme; in the course of its work, NICE will identify gaps in knowledge which the R&D programme will address. The core role of NICE is to deliver Stages 3 and 4 and to absorb the outputs of Stage 6. The processes of Stage 5 are described later.

Box 4.5   The six key stages of consistent standards

- **Stage 1: Identification**
    - for new health interventions – scanning the horizon for new drugs, devices and procedures which are likely to have an impact
    - for existing interventions – examining current practice to identify unjustified variations in use, or uncertainty about effectiveness

- **Stage 2: Evidence collection**
    - undertaking research to assess the clinical and cost-effectiveness of health interventions

- **Stage 3: Appraisal and guidance**
    - carefully considering the implications for clinical practice of the evidence on clinical and cost-effectiveness and producing guidance for the NHS

- **Stage 4: Dissemination**
  - of the guidance and supporting audit methodologies
- **Stage 5: Implementation**
  - at a local level, through clinical governance
- **Stage 6: Monitoring**
  - the impact and keeping advice under review, taking into account the views of patients and their representatives and relevant new research findings

National audits

It was proposed in the White Paper that NICE might take over the running of the four national clinical audits (Box 4.6) and this is confirmed in *A First Class Service*. Of more importance than the minor benefits from central coordination of the four audits is the mandatory participation of all professionals in these audits. Currently, participation varies from 20 to 80%; in future, 100% is

Box 4.6   National confidential enquiries

- National Confidential Enquiry into Perioperative Deaths (NCEPOD) covering deaths within 30 days of an operation (commenced 1988)

- Confidential Enquiry into Stillbirths and Deaths in Infancy (CESDI) identifying ways of preventing early deaths and research needs (commenced 1991)

- Confidential Enquiry into Maternal Deaths (CEMD) assesses trends and causes of death within a year of childbirth (commenced 1951)

- Confidential Inquiry into Suicide and Homicide by People with Mental Illness (CISH) to make recommendations to ministers on clinical practice and policy to reduce such deaths (commenced 1991)

required and non-participation may well be regarded as a disciplinary issue.

Dissemination and monitoring

It is also anticipated that NICE will take the lead role in disseminating authorised guidance to the NHS, a process which has proved challenging in the past. It is supposed to provide a single reference point for all information on standards and audit methods. In practice, the world is awash with standards and audit software and NICE will simply become the government's agent in this field.

The NHS R&D programme has funded research into the dissemination and implementation of evidence-based practice and this will substantially link with the new responsibilities allocated to NICE. What is clear, however, is that nothing will be left to chance; for each NICE guideline published, a formal implementation programme will be demanded of every relevant health organisation, with clinical governance leads expected to police implementation and to ensure success. The Institute itself will not monitor this phase of the work; the CHI and the NFAP will cover these aspects.

The structure and function of NICE

The Institute is established as a Special Health Authority, accountable to the Secretary of State for Health. Sir Michael Rawlins was appointed as chairman early in 1999 and advertisements were placed for non-executive directors, attracting 700 applications. Professor Tony Culyer, a distinguished health economist and architect of the funding system for NHS R&D, will be vice chairman. All board members are ministerial appointments; the chief executive, recruited from St George's Hospital in London, will be accountable to the board.

In addition to the board, a political body, there will be a so-called Partners' Council, representing all the stakeholders (patients, health professions, academics, NHS service interests, pharmaceutical industry) and also appointed by the Secretary of State. The Partners' Council will have up to 46 members. Initially, the secretariat will be provided by the DoH. However, as in the case of the R&D strategy, NICE will want to establish its own identity and style and must therefore create its own staff culture as it seeks to distance itself from the functions it is taking over, replacing them with new vehicles of its own making. The initial brief will be to take over, manage and review the existing functions of the DoH in the production of guidance (Box 4.7).

In essence, the funding available to NICE will come from these sources. No additional funding is promised and little can be expected. It is not yet clear if the £10 million identified in the Modernisation Fund for NICE includes any new money or is wholly a redesignation of previous DoH spending. In short, NICE will not offer new activity, it will simply make sense and value out of the disconnected shambles which constitutes the DoH's efforts in this field in the past.

Box 4.7 Existing Department of Health investment in functions to be transferred to NICE

- the National Prescribing Centre appraisals and bulletins of new and existing drug treatments

- the *Prescriber's Journal*, a short publication for prescribing doctors

- *Effective Health Care* bulletins commissioned through the Centre for Reviews and Dissemination on behalf of the R&D Strategy and the DoH

- the National Centre for Clinical Audit, a partnership between various professional organisations

- PRODIGY, a computer-aided decision-support system for GPs to aid prescribing

- other DoH expenditure on national guidelines and professional audit programmes

National Service Frameworks

The use of NSFs to shape and improve health services in a consistent manner has been described in Part 3 in terms of their role in the development of HImPs. The frameworks will set standards and define service models, lead to programmes to support implementation and include performance measures against which progress can be measured. They will define where, as well as what, care should be provided and, if emerging cancer guidance is anything to go by, will be increasingly centralising of specialist healthcare. The shape and content of each framework is described in *A First Class Service*

Box 4.8   The chapters of a National Service Framework

- A definition of the scope of the framework

- The evidence base
  - needs assessment
  - current service performance
  - evidence of clinical and cost-effectiveness
  - significant service gaps and pressures

- National standards of service and the timescales for delivery

- Key interventions (to achieve the standards) and associated costs

- Commissioned work to support implementation
  - appropriate R&D, such as the NHS R&D programme in health technology assessment
  - appraisal
  - bench marks
  - outcome indicators

- Supporting programmes
  - workforce planning and education and training to meet the standards
  - personal and organisational development
  - developing the necessary information

- A performance management framework for the NSF

(Box 4.8). This dictates not only the shape of the framework but demands that it will be long!

In addition to the existing and proposed NSFs, a set of annual frameworks can be expected throughout the next decade. The criteria to inform the selection of topics have been described in *A First Class Service* (Box 4.9).

It is hoped and expected that the driving force for determining the priorities will be the Annual Report of the government's Chief Medical Officer, focusing on the reduction of inequalities in health.

Box 4.9 Criteria for future National Service Frameworks

- demonstrable relevance to the government's agenda for health improvement and reducing inequalities

- an important health issue (mortality, morbidity, disability, cost)

- an area of public concern

- evidence of a shortfall between actual and acceptable practice

- an area where care may be provided in more than one setting

- an area where reorganisation or restructuring of services is required to ensure service improvement

- a problem which requires new, innovative approaches

Clinical governance

Clinical governance, defined in Box 2.11, is at the centre of the quality agenda, and its successful development and delivery is essential to the overall success of the initiative. In helping to ensure dependable local delivery of healthcare, clinical governance seeks to improve the level of quality of the average health organisation while attempting to eradicate the service failures among the least successful and effective providers and involving effective learning and dissemination from the excellent services at the leading edge of practice. The initial emphasis (in the White Paper) on NHS trusts has been extended to cover primary care and the NHS as a whole with equal force.

Detailed, and surprisingly helpful, guidance was published in March 1999 on the implementation of clinical governance. It covers health authorities, NHS trusts, PCGs and primary care trusts. Further guidance will follow for the dental, optometry and pharmacy professions in primary care but all will be covered, and it is a responsibility of the health authority to pull together all the approaches into a coherent strategy across all local health services. The inclusion of the private and independent sector-provided health services is not within the control of the government at this stage but for important conditions, such as those covered by NSFs, engagement with NHS clinical governance regimes could become a condition of registration. Linkages between local action plans for the implementation of clinical governance and the HImPs are required and the whole scenario is underpinned by the statutory duty for quality included in the Health Act for Trusts (NHS and Primary Care).

While acknowledging that clinical governance is a long-term agenda, the guidance includes specific short- (Box 4.10) and medium- (Box 4.11) term targets and aspirations. These apply to all types of trusts.

Box 4.10   The four key steps to be undertaken by April 2000

- **Establishing leadership, accountability and working arrangements:** By April 1999, health authorities, PCGs, primary care trusts (there won't be any!) and NHS trusts should have identified lead clinicians for clinical governance and set up appropriate structures. For NHS trusts, arrangements should include board subcommittees for overseeing clinical governance

- **The baseline assessment of capability and capacity:** Baseline assessments should be completed by the end of September 1999. NHS trusts and health authorities should agree with their Regional Office a process and timescale for conducting these baseline assessments. Primary care trusts (there still won't be any!) and PCGs should agree similar assessments with their health authority

- **Formulating and agreeing the development plan:** NHS organisations should produce and begin to implement an agreed development plan for clinical governance locally. The plan should include the activities and timescale for closing gaps identified in performance, developing infrastructure, staff and board development, planning and prioritisation, and milestones to assist in assessing achievement. For trusts and health authorities, monitoring of the plan should form part of existing performance management processes. For PCGs and primary care trusts, a process for progress reporting should be agreed with the health authority

- **Clarifying reporting arrangements:** Organisations should ensure that they have appropriate mechanisms in place to deliver routine board reports on progress made in implementing clinical governance. Health authorities, PCGs, primary care trusts and NHS trusts should produce annual reports on what they are doing to improve and maintain clinical quality

Box 4.11　The vision for the next five years

For clinical governance to be successful, all health organisations must demonstrate features such as:

- an open and participative culture in which education, research and the sharing of good practice are valued and expected

- a commitment to quality that is shared by staff and managers, and supported by clearly identified local resources, both human and financial

- a tradition of active working with patients, users, carers and the public

- an ethos of multidisciplinary team working at all levels in the organisation

- regular board-level discussion of all major quality issues for the organisation and strong leadership from the top
- good use of information to plan and to assess progress

Revisiting the official definition of clinical governance (Box 2.11), we can see how the philosophy is being transformed into an action plan:

a framework *for action* of accountability *through the chief executives of NHS trusts and the chairs of primary care groups* for improving the quality *of care* by safeguarding high standards *determined by NICE, NSF's and the Commission for Health Improvement and by reducing variations in treatment and outcomes* and creating an environment in which excellence flourishes *by seeking and securing continuous improvement.*

An integrated approach to clinical governance requires four main building blocks (coherence, infrastructure, quality methods and organisational culture) and two outcome mechanisms for dealing with risk avoidance and poor performance of professional staff (Box 4.12).

The key to success lies in the creation of a new culture in NHS organisations. However, there is no magic trick which changes culture, especially in large organisations with lots of prima-donna professionals. The strategy for quality is therefore based on a set of tasks that will ensure actions and behaviours compatible with the desired culture change. Of special importance is the interaction between the development of clinical governance and the other major cultural changes introduced by *The New NHS*, such as the HImP, the Human Resource Strategy, *Information for Health* and the extension of the NHS R&D programme into the field of organisation and delivery of services and the application of the outputs from the Programme into clinical practice through NICE. In addition to existing national infrastructures such as the Cochrane Library and the NHS Centre for Reviews and Dissemination, a new National Electronic Library for Health is to be established

Box 4.12   The building blocks of clinical governance

- **Building coherence**
  - forging partnerships with external organisations (medical Royal Colleges, NICE), welcoming help and removing barriers to advice
  - excellent internal communications, usually matched by external communications, creating a democratic, open and two-way communications system
  - horizontal dynamism, aligning individual, team and organisational goals

- **Building infrastructure**
  - disseminating information to change power structures by destroying hierarchies created by the hoarding of information
  - using information technology to support practice
  - free and open access to the evidence base for improving practice
  - training and development strategies for all staff
  - allowing time, space and money for the planning and implementation of quality improvements

- **Building quality methods**
  - copy, and systematically disseminate, best practice
  - use the highest quality evidence to help formulate clinical policies
  - actively learn from the lessons of failure, both locally and elsewhere
  - integrate the systems and processes for service improvements

- **Building a new culture**
  - an open and participative management style
  - clear, sensitive and responsive leadership
  - placing a high value on learning and on participation in, and using the results of, research
  - building active partnerships with patients and their representatives
  - creating an ethos of teamwork throughout the organisation

> **Securing the key outcomes**
>
> - **Dealing with risk**
>   - guaranteeing a safe working and intellectual environment, tolerating opinions and celebrating truth and honesty
>   - clarity of procedures, effectiveness of their dissemination, implementation and monitoring for all staff
>   - ensuring all staff are properly trained to do all that is expected of them
>
> - **Dealing with poor performance**
>   - feedback for all staff on their individual and team performances
>   - early recognition of failing individuals or teams
>   - effective and decisive intervention for those who are failing, encompassing training, discipline or dismissal
>   - promoting effective professional self-regulation, preferably team-based

(announced in *Information for Health*). The purpose of the electronic library is to complete the final step between the generation of evidence of importance to services and clinical care and its transmission to the key decision makers.

The greatest concern for the professions lies in mysterious statements like 'applying the lessons of failure' and 'dealing with poor practitioner performance'. Although the guidance document refers specifically to 'moving away from a culture of blame to one of learning', that is not the style of this government and is hard to sustain with such a voracious and often pernicious press and litigious public.

Much more will be written and said about clinical governance in the years to come. It is sufficiently obtuse for major changes in content and purpose to be accommodated and also for it to be discretely marginalised if the public agenda improbably shifts. The probability, however, is that the development and application of clinical governance will grow steadily in importance during the next five to ten years with the creation of new professional roles at the top of organisations and a surge in litigation on the back of the honesty and openness which is a necessary accompaniment to the process. Those who observe that most complainants seek only apology and explanation underestimate the potential for greed.

Once established, it is unlikely that this process can be reversed; nor should it be. By installing responsibility at the heart of the NHS bureaucracy, and spilling over into the public domain through public board reports, clinical governance will soon become just another of the things that management does and only when things go wrong with the process will it really start to have an impact. The guidance describes the roles and responsibilities at every level of the NHS (Box 4.13) in 'bureauspeak'; indeed the organisational focus of responsibility, while ensuring the sort of attention to the process which is the nature of bureaucracy, also detracts from the clinical service focus which ought to be at the heart of clinical governance.

The complex and challenging processes which make up the agenda for clinical governance constitute the greatest opportunity

---

Box 4.13 Organisational roles and responsibilities for clinical governance

- **Health authorities**
    - identify the priorities for quality improvement through the needs assessment phase of the HImP
    - determine investment and action in the HImP to secure agreed improvements in quality
    - recognise and promote good practice
    - support and facilitate the development of clinical governance in all local NHS organisations but especially in PCGs and other contractor professions
    - identify specialties and services which have insufficient critical mass to undertake clinical governance on a local basis and ensure adequate arrangements
    - ensure good clinical governance of health authority functions, such as public health, communicable disease control, clinical advice and health needs assessment

● **Primary care groups**
  - undertake the four key implementation steps (Box 4.10) for clinical governance
  - integrating clinical governance into the development of PCGs
  - assuming joint accountability for the clinical governance of services which are delivered on a multisector, multiagency basis
  - establishing an open, learning relationship, with bodies which may make judgements about the quality of their services or their programme of clinical governance, especially the CHI
  - making sure that clinical governance principles are applied to services delivered by other providers on their behalf through long-term service agreements and through contracts with non-NHS providers
  - developing a coherent approach to clinical governance by working with other agencies, including NHS bodies
  - supporting member practitioners in applying clinical governance to the delivery of GMS and in PCAPs

● **Primary care trusts (when established)**
  as for primary care groups plus
  - ensuring that clinical governance principles are developed and applied to cover the full range of services they provide or are provided by others on their behalf

● **NHS trusts**
  as for primary care groups plus
  - make sure that clinical governance principles are applied to services delivered by other providers on their behalf and in private practice areas of their own facilities
  - ensure all hospital doctors take part in national clinical audits and confidential enquiries

● **NHS Executive Regional Offices**
  - ensure the coherent implementation of all guidance
  - assess year-on-year progress against individual organisation's objectives for the implementation of the four key steps, the vision and the main components of clinical governance
  - facilitate links between the CHI and NHS organisations; help

NHS bodies to make the best use of CHI and to develop and implement action plans following CHI reviews/investigations

- **Commission for Health Improvement**
  as described in **A First Class Service**
  - provide national leadership to develop and disseminate clinical governance principles
  - independently scrutinise local clinical governance arrangements to support, promote and deliver high-quality services, through a rolling programme of local reviews of service providers
  - undertake a programme of service reviews to monitor national implementation of NSFs and review progress locally on implementation of these frameworks and NICE guidance
  - help the NHS to identify and tackle serious or persistent clinical problems. The Commission will have the capacity for rapid investigation and intervention to help put these right
  - over time, increasingly take on responsibility for overseeing and assisting with external incident enquiries

and the biggest threat for the medical profession. Although the language of government documents makes it clear that clinical governance applies to all the professions, in practice, it only has the means to monitor the process for doctors, whose behaviour has led to its evolution.

Reflecting on all the above, it is possible to discern some of the fundamentals for clinical governance and its prospects. The most important factor in its long-term development is the amount of political commitment placed behind it. Without political priority, the necessary investment in infrastructure will not be made and the empowerment of leaders will be lost. The effectiveness of the inspection and regulation process is also important. Consistency of standards and approach is critical to secure the reputation of the new Commission and to avoid the pitfalls which befell OFSTED in its early years and continue to dog its credibility. Perhaps the most contentious aspect of clinical governance is the way in which it transfers accountability for clinical performance from the individual to the organisation. This is exceptional enough for hospital doctors, but it is revolutionary for general practice. Herein lies the real challenge and the approach has to be suitably sensitive. The nature of leadership required to handle such a paradigm shift is comprehensively misunderstood by both politicians and officials. While the motivation of leaders must be positive and corporate, one must question whether it is wise to over-personalise the leadership role, as is required. Securing the right balance between managerialism and clinical independence necessitates leadership which is broadly based but clearly located. Doctors are generally very bad at teamworking, partly because they are trained to be individuals and partly because egos and teamworking do not normally blend. Even within practices, partners tend to be isolated. The shift from this to group responsibility, for clinical governance and most of the other tasks of PCGs, is a leap in the pitch dark, hence the risks and the long time frame (at least for clinical governance). I suspect that health authorities will recognise the risk and will adopt a quite different approach to clinical governance in primary care – based on nurturing, supporting and enabling – to that in secondary care, which will resemble performance management. As a corporate responsibility, good leadership of the PCG/trust is a pre-requisite for good leadership of clinical governance; were chairs selected with this in mind? Also, however good the leadership is, who is going to capture the hearts and minds?

Everything the health authority does for the PCG – such as securing ownership of the HImP and supporting the group to develop and deliver its responsibilities – the PCG must do for each of its practices. Not only does the group not have the physical or financial resources to do this but there is no precedent for anything like this. Many LMCs have expressed a desire to be involved in clinical governance arrangements. They are scarcely mentioned in any of the guidance, largely because they have no constituents who are not covered by the PCGs. Nonetheless, they can have a role in helping to manage the consequences of the mature process, especially in helping to deal with poorly performing doctors. It is desirable therefore to find a way of involving the LMC in some mechanism adjacent to the clinical governance systems so that they are able to help and do not feel disfranchised; nonetheless, it has little to do with them really.

Lifelong learning and professional self-regulation

Supporting clinical governance in the establishment of local systems for quality improvement are a framework for continuing professional development (CPD), or lifelong learning, and strengthened professional self-regulation at national level (*see* Box 4.14 for definitions). In both cases, these mechanisms constitute the interface between local management of the professions and national independence as professions. This has long been an area of conflict, though almost always concealed, and open disagreements usually went the way of the professional body. The relationship between professional leadership and the government has traditionally been

---

Box 4.14   Continuing professional development

A process of lifelong learning for all individuals and teams which meets the needs of patients and delivers the health outcomes and healthcare priorities of the NHS and which enables professionals to expand and fulfil their potential.

CPD follows a circular pathway through assessment of needs, planning for personal development, implementation and evaluation of the effectiveness of CPD and of benefit to patient care.

Professional self-regulation

Gives health professionals the ability to set their own standards of professional practice, conduct and discipline. To justify this freedom and maintain the trust of patients, the professions must be openly accountable for the standards they set, taking account of legitimate public expectations and the realities of local service delivery, and the way these are enforced.

Systems of professional self-regulation must be strengthened, to restore public confidence, to ensure that they are:

- open to public scrutiny

- responsive to changing clinical practice and service needs

- publicly accountable for professional standards set nationally, and the action taken to maintain these standards

handled with kid gloves. Whatever the private thoughts of ministers and officials, the risks of hostile engagement have always been regarded as too high to contemplate. The current proposals do not significantly depart from this line but the relative vulnerability of the medical profession, in the aftermath of highly publicised failures, has allowed the government to demand more than usual and encouraged the profession to respond positively to these overtures.

Further guidance on lifelong learning is expected early in 2000 and professional organisations have responded with orgasmic vigour to the government's challenge to tighten their standards of professional practice. As with so many other aspects of standard setting and regulation, it is the policing of the standards which presents the challenge. The legalistic structures and processes of the GMC are a massive obstacle to delivering prompt and effective action in dealing with doctors whose performance causes concern. The GMC's record to date is lamentable and, despite significant expansion governing the rules of access and reasons for referral, it remains as big a part of the problem as a part of the solution.

The work which remains to be done on lifelong learning entails mainly practical issues (Box 4.15) and the development of links to other components of the government's comprehensive strategies encompassed by *The New NHS*.

Box 4.15 Practical issues in developing lifelong learning

- the role of monitoring, peer review and appraisal

- the role of new technology and distance learning in maximising learning opportunities and customising the process

- how the expertise of professional and statutory bodies can best support local CPD, within the context of clinical governance

- the educational infrastructure required to identify and meet CPD needs

The Commission for Health Improvement

The establishment of the Commission may not be the most inventive development in the government's programme but it is one of the most important. Its main brief is to provide independent scrutiny of local efforts to improve quality and to help address any serious problems; the core functions are described at the end of Box 4.13.

The Commission's establishment requires primary legislation (see Part 6) and therefore will not be fully functioning until early 2000. This is considerably later than hoped for; original performance objectives for the NHS included an expectation that at least 40 site visits will have been conducted by the end of 2000. While such targets may yet be set and met, the absence of any infrastructure (it cannot commence until after Royal Assent for the Health Bill), inspectors or routines for visiting and evaluating make such a programme pointless rather than daunting.

I was recently discussing career options with a NHS Executive high flyer and asked him to consider which would be the most important and influential post in the NHS in ten years' time. It is at least possible, based on the experience in education, that the Director (or equivalent) of the Commission will justify such a description. The central importance of the Commission lies not so much in its core role, more in that it is an independent national organisation with direct access to ministers and a high public profile. The rather dry tasks it will conduct (Box 4.16) pale compared with the potential impact it can have on policy and the future of individual organisations. The major management task for NHS and primary care trusts will be preparing for a visit by the Commission.

As proposed in *The New NHS*, any NHS organisation can summon the help of the Commission in investigating local concerns about the quality of care or individual and team performance (Box 2.13). Even in such cases, the responsibility for following up reports will rest with local and regional organisations. In the event of delay, or a failure of local organisations to address problems, the Secretary of State may ask the Commission to step in. Since this would be the most undesirable of processes, health authorities, PCGs and NHS and primary care trusts will be well advised to

Box 4.16 What the Commission for Health Improvement will do

- Conduct regular planned and announced visits to NHS and primary care trusts every 3–4 years to provide an external and independent check on local arrangements for implementing clinical governance

- Follow through the publication of guidance from NICE and the recommendations in NSFs with a review of local implementation, including national surveys of implementation and compliance with the guidance

- Endorse external audit programmes in which all hospital doctors will have to participate

- Review a trust's response to other external audit processes (such as the Health Service Ombudsman) and the processes and results of internal enquiries, including individual clinician performance data

- Publish a summary of their findings

- Identify action plans for trusts and their Regional Office to take forward but also follow up specific recommendations for action itself

- Include primary care provision and commissioning agencies (PCGs and health authorities) in the course of reviews if their actions are thought to be affecting service quality

- Take over the work of the Clinical Standards Advisory Group

- Work closely with the Audit Commission to develop a coordinated joint work programme

- Support health authorities and Regional Offices in the investigation of poor performance in NHS trusts

involve the Commission at an early stage in their own investigations, even if on an informal basis.

It is still proposed that the Commission will, 'over time', take over responsibility for external incident enquiries initiated by local NHS bodies. The lack of direction on this point suggests that there remains some uncertainty about the wisdom of this move and it could lead to the Commission being excessively identified with critical reports at an early stage in its development.

Ministers are still exploring the options for the future regulation of the independent acute sector, perhaps taking on powers initially to apply their principles to independent providers which provide a significant proportion of their services to NHS patients, such as specialist private mental health units.

As seen in Box 3.29, a sum of £3 million has been identified in the Modernisation Fund to set up the Commission. However, it is possible that this sum includes some or all of the current investment in similar activities funded by the DoH, such as the Clinical Standards Advisory Group and HAS2000. As the Commission's work matures, and relationships with local NHS bodies develop constructively, it is anticipated that an increasing proportion of Commission income will come direct from work commissioned by local agencies. Major enquiries will continue to be funded locally but it is expected that the Commission's involvement will lead to greater economy in their conduct.

As is the case with similar national independent organisations such as OFSTED, the Commission will publish an annual report

---

Box 4.17 How the Commission for Health Improvement will help patients

The Commission ... will provide an independent reassurance to patients that effective systems are in place to deliver high quality services throughout the NHS. It will ... offer rapid support where there is a need to help local NHS organisations resolve particularly difficult problems. The Commission has an important role in working to reduce variations in services across the NHS through its systematic reviews of services, providing feedback into the NSFs, and its monitoring of the uptake of NICE guidance.

describing the progress being made, especially in the development of clinical governance. The board of the Commission will include a wide range of stakeholders but they will be present on their individual merits, not as representatives. A lay chair was proposed originally but the position has been given to Dame Dierdre Hine, formerly CMO for Wales. Peter Hamer, the waiting list supremo, has been appointed as Director. The construction and breadth of review teams has yet to be determined but will cover a wide range of expertise including clinical, managerial and lay members. The tools of inspection and the means and style of reporting have also yet to be fully developed. The legislation will focus the Commission's brief and style on improving services for patients (Box 4.17).

The national framework for assessing performance

The six dimensions of the framework were shown in Box 2.17. After extensive consultation and road-testing of the indicators proposed in *The New NHS*, the NHS Performance Assessment Framework for application in 1999/2000 was published in April 1999. The fundamental purpose of such a framework is to be used to improve health and enhance the quality of care and the health outcomes for patients. Road-testing was used to ensure that these purposes were adequately addressed by the indicators selected for use. The indicators are generally indirect measures of quality, but may be used to draw attention to issues requiring action. Local NHS organisations must use the six areas of the framework in drawing up the HImP and in developing robust clinical governance processes.

The road tests covered areas such as the assessment of local cancer services, mental health services, learning disability services and services for the elderly, developing the HImP and involving the public. The main messages from this, and from the consultation, were the need for a wider focus on performance and the use of comparative information to facilitate benchmarking. Some consultees proposed the inclusion of a seventh key area based on human resources but this would be out of kilter with the others which are all concerned with outcomes for patients.

The long set of proposed high-level indicators (*see* Box 2.18) has been revised (and reduced) in the light of consultation. Certain proposed indicators have been rightly dropped altogether (e.g. district nurse contacts), some have been revised and others included for the first time to reflect the national priorities in *Our Healthier Nation*. Interface indicators are included to initiate the assessment of whole system service performance embracing both health and social services. Overall, the framework of indicators will facilitate assessment of performance across a range of dimensions (Box 4.18) and will be further developed to enable benchmarking of both health authorities and NHS trusts.

Box 4.18   The dimensions of performance assessment and examples for analysis

- population group
  - geographical area, ethnic group, social class

- condition/client group
  - coronary heart disease, asthma and chronic respiratory disease, children

- service organisation
  - health authority, NHS trust, PCG

The framework will play a major part in developing and clarifying accountability arrangements between key agencies in *The New NHS* (Box 4.19).

In the future, the framework will incorporate the linked work being done on NHS trust reference costs (first published in November 1998), the set of clinical indicators and clinical effectiveness indicators (some included in the initial set of high-level indicators; Box 4.20), primary care effectiveness indicators and the results of the first survey of NHS patients (completed in early 1999).

The elimination of inappropriate variations in NHS performance remains one of the government's key objectives, in order to secure fairness, equity and to release resources from the inefficient use of

Box 4.19 The NHS Performance Assessment Framework and formal accountability

- **The Health Improvement Programme**
  - identifying targets for measurable improvement across the six areas of the framework
  - targets for improvement quantified via service and financial frameworks, including plans to meet baseline requirements (emergency pressures, financial balance, waiting lists, etc.)

- **Annual accountability agreements**
  - between a health authority and its PCGs containing key targets, objectives and standards
  - consistent with national priorities and the HImP
  - progress assessed in the context of the framework using high-level performance indicators and local information

- **Service agreements**
  - between health authorities/PCGs and NHS trusts
  - patient- and service-based and developed at clinical directorate level
  - each agreement to have jointly owned measures of performance linked to targets and monitored in line with the framework

- **NHS/social care interface**
  - jointly monitored by NHS Executive Regional Offices and the Social Services Inspectorate
  - indicators common to the NHS high-level performance indicators and the indicators for personal service indicators
  - help promote common understanding and ownership of performance at the interface between services

- **Annual performance agreements**
  - between each health authority and its Regional Office covering key objectives for the year
  - plans for the development of local NHS organisations and the plans in the service and financial framework
  - assess the influence of plans on performance across the six areas of the framework

Box 4.20   The high-level indicator set in 1999/2000
(*see also* Box 2.19)

- **Health improvement**
  - deaths from all causes (for people aged 15–64)
  - deaths from all causes (for people aged 65–74)
  - cancer registrations
  - deaths from malignant neoplasms (linked to reductions target in *Our Healthier Nation* and the objectives in the National Priorities Guidance)
  - deaths from all circulatory diseases (linked as above)
  - suicide rates (linked as above)
  - deaths from accidents (linked as above)

- **Fair access**
  - surgery rates (National Priorities Guidance)
  - size of inpatient waiting list per head of population (weighted) amended for 1999/2000 following consultation and road test
  - adults registered with an NHS dentist (amended as above)
  - children registered with an NHS dentist (amended as above)
  - early detection of cancer (National Priorities Guidance)

- **Effective delivery of appropriate healthcare**
  - disease prevention and health promotion (National Priorities Guidance and amended following consultation and road test)
  - early detection of cancer (National Priorities Guidance)
  - inappropriately used surgery
  - surgery rates (National Priorities Guidance)
  - acute care management (amended as above)
  - chronic care management (amended as above)
  - mental health in primary care (amended as above)
  - cost-effective prescribing
  - discharge from hospital (clinical indicator and personal social services indicator)

- **Efficiency**
  - day case rate
  - length of stay in hospital (case-mix adjusted)
  - unit cost of maternity (adjusted and amended as above)

- unit cost of caring for patients in receipt of specialist mental health services (adjusted and amended as above)
- generic prescribing

- **Patient/carer experience of the NHS**
  - patients who wait less than two hours for emergency admission through A&E
  - patients with operation cancelled for non-medical reasons
  - delayed discharge from hospital for people aged 75 or over (personal social services indicator)
  - first outpatient appointments for which patient did not attend
  - outpatients seen within 13 weeks of GP referral (National Priorities Guidance)
  - percentage of those on waiting list waiting 12 months or more (National Priorities Guidance and amended as above)

- **Health outcomes of NHS health care**
  - conceptions below age 16 (*Our Healthier Nation*)
  - decayed, missing and filled teeth in 5-year-old children (National Priorities Guidance)
  - adverse events/complications of treatment (clinical indicator)
  - emergency admissions to hospital for people aged 75 and over (National Priorities Guidance and personal social services indicator)
  - emergency psychiatric readmission rate (National Priorities Guidance and personal social services indicator)
  - infant deaths
  - survival rates for breast and cervical cancer (National Priorities Guidance)
  - avoidable deaths
  - in-hospital premature deaths (clinical indicator)

facilities and time. The benchmarking of a wide range of comparative performance data is seen as the core of this approach and proposals are being developed to improve the quality and range of information to promote this. Further detailed information on the approach is expected during the next two years.

National survey of patient and user experience

Since its launch, in October 1998, the national survey has run into deep trouble over routine ethical and data protection issues. The survey is intended to complement other measures of NHS performance by providing a mixture of hard and soft data about public confidence in, and patient experiences of, the NHS in order to inform local and national policy and action. Hitherto, surveys of public opinion of the NHS were commissioned by organisations with a clear vested interest in specific outcomes, mainly political (small 'p' intended). The National Survey will provide a consistent, NHS-owned but externally, scientifically and professionally conducted assessment of patients' experiences and public expectations and is intended to produce information which will be of help to patients (Box 4.21).

Box 4.21   A survey of patients to help patients

- enable local managers and health professionals to take direct account of patients' and users' concern so as to improve services

- provide bench marks against which patient experiences locally can be assessed, and highlighting the potential for improvement

- demonstrating to patients and users that their views on services are important

---

The survey was commissioned from a consortium headed by Social and Community Planning Research, together with Picker Europe Ltd and the Imperial College School of Medicine. These organisations offer a full range of experience and expertise required to carry out this type of survey.

As primary research, approval had to be given by the Medical Research Ethics Committee, a time-consuming process, and several parties raised the issue of data protection since the survey relied on the use of data (diagnosis of heart disease or cancer) for a purpose other than that for which it was collected. The general population survey was conducted at the end of 1998/beginning of 1999, covering 1000 people in each health authority in England. The survey will therefore provide a national picture with 0.2% of the population invited to participate, and a snapshot of local experience to compare with the national position. After eventually satisfying the needs of the Data Protection Registrar, the survey of hospital patients with coronary heart disease finally got under way in March 1999, with voluntary participation by relevant NHS trusts. The survey of cancer patients proved more challenging and has been postponed with the intention of completely redesigning the proposed survey and commencing no earlier than late 1999. These experiences may well lead to the government rethinking both the logistics and purpose of these surveys with the possibility of considerably less ambitious and more locally owned variations being adopted in due course. This would be a shame as reliable national surveys are the only way to generate truly comparative data.

Part 5

Primary care

Introduction

As with the reforms of the previous government, primary care finds itself at the heart of radical change in the NHS once again. The principal reason lies in the reality, supported by government recognition, that very little can change in the NHS unless primary care is closely involved. Just as fundholding was created in 1991 to stimulate the NHS internal market, PCGs now exist to encourage and reinforce the integration of community-based health and social care services.

'W(h)ither the independent practitioner'

Every reorganisation of the NHS brings with it concerns among GPs that their independent contractor status is under threat. It has so far survived not only the first 50 years of the NHS but also the creation of the NHS itself. The assurances given to GPs about the retention of their independence in this White Paper are of uncertain security. It is known that Treasury analysis suggests that the current arrangements for resourcing primary care are not a particularly bad deal for public funding. Despite the natural resistance to private enterprise in the NHS, the independent contractor status has survived successive Labour and Conservative administrations which have done their best to control the professions in many ways. It is certainly possible that this government will take advantage of its own strength and the lack of opposition to its NHS proposals to have a go at independent contractor status as never before, though probably not in this parliament.

The NHS (Primary Care) Act 1997, passed by the previous government, provides a legislative basis on which to initiate pilots involving the direct employment of GPs. Further measures have been introduced since the election to allow the employment of GP principals to address certain service deficiencies and to fill temporary gaps in services to patients. Where recruitment of principals has traditionally been difficult, due to the excessive cost of buying-in to expensively propertied practices mainly in inner-city areas, direct employment could become a common feature of primary care in both medicine and dentistry.

Primary care trusts hold the key

The establishment of PCGs, leading to primary care trust status, offers a wider range of incentives and opportunities for change. By integrating commissioning budgets, prescribing costs and cash-limited GMS funds, and moving towards equalisation of primary care funding across the country, more resources may be available for primary care than it is possible to spend under the current system in areas where recruitment is difficult and list sizes are high. It is more likely that PCGs will invest these resources in new ways of providing primary care, in order to reduce the burden on themselves, than in adding to secondary care investment, although the insolvency of NHS trusts will impose pressures on them. This could be one of the stimuli to employed principals as the basis of primary care in cities.

It is also becoming clear that the creation of primary care trusts will provide a systematic opportunity to vary the national GMS contract. While there may be small beginnings, there should be plenty of time during the life of this government for local contracts to become the norm. While such changes will have to be negotiated, and will presumably be in the interests of local GPs, the benefits for the service as a whole may well eventually justify the buying out of the national contract.

Why change?

There are several reasons to think that the integrated NHS will benefit from changes in the status of GPs. First, primary care trusts will extend primary care as we know it into a continuum including community care and hospitals. The separateness which the independent contractor status gives GPs is a real obstacle to realising the benefits of integration. It also conferred many advantages, but their importance may now be declining while the enormous and growing burden of chronic disease management in the community demands different values and priorities. Second, the White Paper gives a positive boost to the role of nurses in both primary and secondary care. The numbers, status and independence of nurses in primary care in particular are rising; projections are that nursing will become the most numerous profession in primary care within ten years, even disregarding the community staff employed by NHS trusts. Within the Level 4 primary care trusts, nurses will greatly outnumber doctors (as providers) from the outset. The continued independence of GPs will become increasingly incongruous and the pressure to change will grow.

It may be worth considering whether direct employment of GP principals actually offers any benefits to the NHS when it is far from obvious that direct employment of hospital consultants for 50 years has rendered them obedient and compliant servants of the state. However, it is likely that an employed primary care workforce would help reduce variations in the availability of primary care across the country through the use of direction of labour. Fifty years of the Medical Practices Committee has failed to achieve this and the present government is taking equality of access more seriously than any of its predecessors. It may also be argued that the extension of the clinical governance initiative into primary care is going to be toothless unless practitioners are directly employed. The enforcement of clinical and service standards in primary care is critical to the success of the government's strategy for raising standards and improving quality. It may take the view that the independent contractor status of GP principals is able to sabotage a policy of quality improvement which will have widespread support from the public and other professions; however, all its predecessors have failed in this regard and it is highly presumptive to assume that radical action is likely or indeed, if taken, likely to succeed.

Necessity is the mother of invention

In the fullness of time, politics permitting, we can assume that primary care trusts will renegotiate the GMS contract. A recruitment crisis in primary care, now a real possibility, will hasten the acceptability of such a move. The attractiveness of locally negotiated changes to the national contract will lead to the obsolescence and then the redundancy of the Red Book (the statement of fees and allowances which implements the financial aspects of the contract between GPs and the government of the day). The master plan assumes that this will be a voluntary process, with existing practitioners entitled to retain independent contractor status until they retire. Many would probably be persuaded to transfer to employment if they were offered consultant terms and conditions, a guaranteed (reasonably) high salary and long-term security of income.

The last great restrictive practice

There is a major obstacle to the development of primary care along these lines in rural areas. This concerns the rewards received by dispensing practices and the perverse disincentives which the remuneration system currently offers dispensing doctors against cost-efficient prescribing (the practice receives a fixed proportion of the drug cost as a fee, therefore penalising the practice if it adopts, say, more generic prescribing). This arrangement will have to be renegotiated in a way that protects both the public purse and the continuation of local primary care in rural areas, these smaller practices being dependent on dispensing profits for their economic viability. Conversely, I believe that the integration of prescribing and dispensing provides the ideal model of primary care so long as adequate standards of dispensing practice are met. Eliminating the restrictive practices of dispensing pharmacists may well lead to the decline of the corner shop chemist but, if it leads to integrated primary care, the patient will be the beneficiary.

Primary care groups

GP fundholders were either leaders or followers. The leaders were consonant, believed in the principles of fundholding, campaigned for the retentions of its freedoms and flexibility, and vigorously defended its advantages; the followers were dissonant, were uncomfortable with the principles, became fundholders because the option of not doing so was threatening to them and their patients, and were content with the prospect of a return to a more collective approach to local service planning. Non-fundholders were also of two types: some rejected the principles so profoundly that they declined all pressure and incentive to join the scheme; others were simply disconnected from the world of the NHS market and never saw the need to become involved. The only real problem is that all these types of GPs are now expected to work together for the mutual benefit of all their patients in PCGs. The lead has tended to be taken by former fundholders wishing to retain influence, but previously excluded practitioners have also emerged as new power brokers.

A new start

In all respects, PCGs are new organisations, not a replacement for fundholding or the extension of total purchasing pilot projects. They are collective, geographical arrangements of community and primary care staff, led initially by GPs and community nurses. They will both provide services and commission them, the vertical integration enjoyed by district health authorities prior to the reforms of the previous government enhanced by the horizontal integration of the first contact services, including housing and social care. They look very much like a transitional arrangement between the era of the internal market with the primary care-led NHS and the independence of the small business in health, and the age of collectivism in a modern society. In this latter vision, people and organisations work together for a common good but in a manner which is subject to external review and contestability, where good performance is rewarded and poor performance is not tolerated. This is a noble and ambitious goal and not one which has ever been achieved in peacetime, and only exceptionally in wartime, by English-speaking peoples.

Managing primary care

Two important features of PCGs are not yet fully worked through. First, they are accountable to health authorities for their delivery of the HImP, but are they equally accountable as providers? The active management of primary care is the one missing element in all previous NHS structures; these proposals provide, for the first time, an appropriate framework for peer-led management of GMS and related primary care and community services. Second, local democracy continues to be excluded from the NHS, although local elected members (of local authorities) are likely to have an increased presence on the boards of NHS trusts and health authorities, though in the latter case possibly in unofficial competition with their own (local authority) chief executives. It is possible that the ultimate manifestation of primary care trusts will be a locally democratic body, providing true local public accountability for any part of the health services for the first time since 1974. However, it is more likely that the government will seize the opportunity to further centralise control through the directly managed NHS.

Sized for integrating service delivery

The average size of PCGs, at around 100 000 population, is arbitrary. It is bigger than any practice and bigger than almost all total purchasing pilots but smaller than all health authorities. They are therefore unlike any existing structure in size and will necessitate new partnerships and relationships to be forged. If service commissioning were the main task of PCGs, the proposed size would be pointless; it has been demonstrated in other countries, e.g. the Netherlands, that a population of at least one million is required for effective commissioning. Of course, it is possible that the British government is adopting pointless policies; it would not be the first time. However, I believe it is not commissioning that is the main agenda, but integration of primary, community and social care. A community of 100000 may be an appropriate basis for service integration. However, the management cost burden will be higher at this size than with larger groups and it must be on the cards for PCGs to merge at about the time that they aspire to primary care trust status. This would bring them close to the average size of a district health authority before 1991.

Social tension

The prospects for integrating social care into this framework are somewhat remote at the present time. Local authority social services have had a trying time in recent years in terms of scandals, funding and priorities. The usual hysterical and self-righteous public and political reaction to service failures by social workers has not abated under new ministers. It is of course tragic when people under care or supervision are abused or killed, but the nature of the work and the clients requires some risks to be taken and some failures are inevitable. The culture of blaming does a disservice to social work professionals and is also dishonest to the community, implying wrongly that all service failures are avoidable and that therefore someone must be blamed. The transfer of social services to non-political accountability is unlikely to be acceptable but the desire for service integration of care of the elderly and mentally ill is strong enough for some bold moves. It is, for example, possible for all children's services in local authorities to be integrated into a single department, including education and child protection. It is probable that NHS and social services mental health services and budgets will be integrated in some experimental pilot projects, as promoted in *Partnership in Action*. The real challenge comes with elderly care, the biggest slice of both health and social care, and the main target for primary and community care integration.

The paradox of practice-level change

Perhaps the greatest challenge of all for PCGs is the marriage of collectivism and the achievement of improvements at practice level. While the end of fundholding will abolish routine practice-level collection of commissioning data, it is precisely these data which will be required to stimulate behaviour change in the use of specialist services and in securing effective service integration. The management resources available to PCGs will not be sufficient to support this if downward pressure on management costs continues to excite politicians. A nice paradox for the next Secretary of State!

The evolution of PCGs and trusts

After long, and publicly acrimonious, negotiations between the representatives of GPs and the government, a measure of agreement was reached in June 1998 and reflected in public correspondence between the parties. The key issues covered by the agreement are described in Box 5.1.

Extensive guidance on the shape, role, activities and establish-

---

Box 5.1   The agreement between the government and the medical profession

- The establishment of PCGs will not affect independent contractor status

- Patients will continue to be guaranteed the drugs, investigations and the treatments they need

- The freedom to refer and prescribe remains unchanged

- GPs have the right to decide locally whether they will be in the majority on PCG boards and the right to have a GP chair should they wish

- GPs who take on responsibilities within PCGs – in their development, governing or management processes – will have their time appropriately remunerated

- The government will ensure that every GP surgery will be connected to the NHSnet and, by 2002, all GP surgeries will be able to receive some hospital test results over the NHSnet

- The government is committed to real-terms increases in resources for the NHS every year

- Every PCG will know (by autumn 1998) what level of resource they have available and how this has been calculated, in accordance with a national needs-based formula to which the General Medical Services Committee has an input

- All GPs will have the opportunity to secure new resources for the practice

- The level of investment in primary care infrastructure will be maintained and uplifted for inflation

- At the earliest legislative opportunity, the government will restore the right of LMCs to represent all GPs (including those covered by personal medical services pilots)

- NHS Executive Regional Offices will ensure that health authorities explicitly provide evidence of the LMC view on their proposals for establishing PCGs; practices which feel disadvantaged can ask the LMC to inform the Regional Office

- For the GP, PCGs provide an opportunity to secure new resources for the practice, the primary healthcare team and for primary care in general

ment of PCGs was published three times, in April, August and December 1998, and was followed in February 1999 by preliminary guidance, in anticipation of the passing of the legislation, on the establishment of primary care trusts.

The first set of guidance dealt with the functions and configuration of PCGs, as described in Part 2 of this book and earlier in this chapter. The second tranche of guidance (HSC 1998/139, Developing Primary Care Groups, August 1998) was advisory but brought much closer to reality the vision of PCGs as the main integrating vehicle in *The New NHS* (Box 5.2). In addition to 32 pages of the HSC, there were a further 45 pages of supporting guidance wherein lay most of the important detail for implementing the new structures and roles.

Box 5.2 Key elements of the advice on developing PCGs (HSC 1998/139)

- **How PCGs will be formed**
  - established as subcommittees of health authorities
  - membership must enjoy the confidence of both stakeholders and health authorities

- **How PCGs will be governed**
  - the board structure ensures that doctors and community nurses are in the lead
  - active social services support for joint approaches to service development
  - the board must be large enough to include a range of skills but small enough to be workable
  - the board will include:
    - 4–7 GPs
    - 1–2 community or practice nurses
    - 1 social services nominee
    - 1 lay member
    - 1 health authority non-executive director
    - 1 PCG chief executive (variously referred to in earlier guidance as chief officer or manager)
  - the board may co-opt other specialists as associate, non-voting members
  - GPs may opt to be in a majority on the board
  - appointments will normally be for up to three years without reselection
  - the board will appoint one of their members to be the chair

---

(other than the chief executive or the health authority non-executive director)
- GPs have the right to decide that one of their number shall be the chair
- while various methods may be used for selecting members of the board, it is expected that they will be representative of their constituency and either elected or appointed through an open process
- members of the board, while bringing specialist skills to their role and representing their peers, will be expected to work corporately and as a team

- **The actions and accountability of PCGs**
  - PCGs are part of the NHS and must comply with national priorities and the HImP
  - as a committee of the health authority, the PCG is accountable through its chair to the chief executive of the health authority
  - the PCG chair will be appointed 'responsible officer' for the delegated budget
  - health authorities will delegate as much responsibility to PCGs as is consistent with their capability and competence
  - the PCG chief executive will be accountable to the PCG chair but remain an employee of the health authority
  - PCGs are responsible for all the patients on the lists of practices covered by the group but also for all residents of the area covered by the practices in the group; these may not be the same and responsibility for commissioning hospital services may be conducted by another PCG in another health authority for some residents
  - PCGs will be bound by the statutory duty of partnership in respect of compliance with the HImP
  - the relationship between the health authority and the PCG will be expressed in an annual accountability agreement
  - PCGs must also be responsive and accountable to their stakeholders through election of board members, public meetings and transparent processes, regular communication, annual accountability agreements and clear and open clinical governance arrangements

- **The operational management of PCGs**
  - health authorities will help PCGs to develop by
    - establishing a framework for corporate governance (e.g. financial control, delegation schedule)
    - acting consistently with the accountability arrangements, including the respective commissioning responsibilities of the PCG and the health authority
    - involving the PCG in the work of the health authority
    - providing some support functions such as public health, finance, information and IT management
    - providing training to the group in involving patients and carers
  - PCGs are expected to work collegiately with others to ensure the best value from the management resources available
  - larger groups may develop subgroups to reflect local concerns
  - each PCG will appoint a senior doctor or nurse to take board responsibility for clinical governance (similarly within each practice)
  - by agreement with the health authority, the group may allocate resources from its unified budget for their own training and development

- **The financial operation of PCGs**
  - the responsibilities of PCGs, in the use of public funds, are to
    - manage within the resources available
    - ensure that resources are best used to benefit patients
    - ensure fairness between practices and patients
    - facilitate prudent financial planning and appropriate delegation of budgets
    - establish risk management strategies with other PCGs and health authorities
    - offer incentives for service development or good performance
    - guarantee at least the 'existing' level of investment in primary care and enhance it when consistent with the HImP

The supporting guidance dealt with a number of important operational issues, such as the clearing house system for minimising redundancy of staff involved in fundholding, the application of statutory redundancy pay for staff employed by practices, the development of stakeholder involvement in the PCG, establishing clinical governance arrangements, health improvement and information management. Many of these were of short-term impact only; others, such as clinical governance, will be of enduring effect. In addition, it describes the ways in which the other contractor professions can be involved in the work of the group, for example dentists in the oral health strategy, optometrists in the care of diabetics, pharmacists in cost-effective prescribing.

Clinical governance in PCGs

Although welcome at the time, this guidance was probably premature, preceding the formal guidance on clinical governance by some seven months. As a result, the enaction of these early proposals are not necessarily consistent with later thinking (described in Part 4). The basic principles of clinical governance in primary care are outlined in Box 5.3.

This agenda is recognised to be professionally and sociologically challenging for primary care professions and the expectations of tight control and accountability are less marked than for hospital clinicians. Over time, however, the same disciplines are likely to be

---

Box 5.3   Clinical governance arrangements in PCGs

- **Principles for the clinical governance process**
  - inclusive – no opting out
  - the topics and the process should gain the confidence of participants
  - focus on improving the many and tackling the unacceptable

- **Aims of the clinical governance process**
  - focus on specific issues
  - designed to secure achievable change
  - reflective and supportive for health professionals

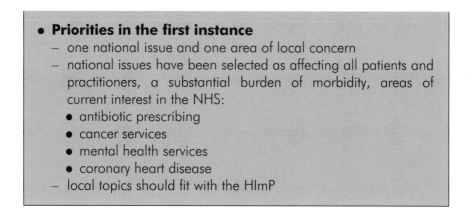

- **Priorities in the first instance**
  - one national issue and one area of local concern
  - national issues have been selected as affecting all patients and practitioners, a substantial burden of morbidity, areas of current interest in the NHS:
    - antibiotic prescribing
    - cancer services
    - mental health services
    - coronary heart disease
  - local topics should fit with the HImP

applied, especially in the context of the forthcoming trust status and especially in efforts to reduce variations in practice in primary care, the focus being on prescribing and on referrals to hospital. It is in these behaviours that NHS resources are committed and in their change that NHS solvency is likely to rely.

Delivering the agenda; governing arrangements

Dual guidance was published in December 1998 on the specific eligibility and roles of PCG board members and long and detailed information on how groups will function in practice. Earlier (in October), separate rules had been produced on the remuneration of chairs and members of PCGs. This clarified the pay and practice reimbursement arrangements for GP and other members (only the health authority non-executive director does not receive pay for his or her PCG role) and set the chair's pay at a level below that of health authority and NHS trust chairs – enabling the chairs of primary care trusts to be agreed at that higher level when legislation permits.

The governing arrangements include a great deal of fine detail which significantly changed the PCG board arrangements in some places. Relevant issues are summarised in Box 5.4.

PCGs will have two statutory functions (health improvement and developing primary and community health services) and one optional function (commissioning hospital and community health

Box 5.4 Eligibility and related issues for PCG board members

● Health authority non-executive members
- may sit on more than one PCG board
- (where the number of non-executives is insufficient) may be replaced by a second lay member, resident in the PCG area
- GPs and registered nurses may not sit as health authority non-executive directors on PCG boards (individuals had to choose which board – HA or PCG – they wished to serve on)

● Nomination of chair
- a member of the board (except the chief executive and the non-executive director)
- the GP constituency may decide to hold the chair, in which case GP members of the board will nominate to the chair
- if no GP is willing to take the chair (or if the GPs decide not to chair the group) the group board will nominate a member to chair
- the health authority will always have the right to reject a nomination and explain fully its reasons for doing so

● General practitioners
- between four and seven GPs may sit on the board
- the definition of GP includes all doctors working in general practice, defence medical services practice and personal medical services pilots
- if fewer than four GPs are willing to fill the board places, vacancies can be filled by a nurse, lay member or local authority officer
- GPs cannot be members of more than one PCG board

● Registered nurses
- may be a nurse, midwife or health visitor
- may be employed by a GP or a NHS trust (so long as their work is mainly community-based)
- a nurse may be on only one PCG board

● Local authority nominated officers
- local authorities with social services responsibilities will nominate an officer to sit on the PCG board

- where the PCG covers more than one social services authority, the authorities must agree which of them is represented on the board
- a social services representative may sit on more than one PCG board

- **Lay members**
  - health authorities should appoint a lay member to the PCG board to represent the interests of the community
  - the lay member must live in the area covered by the PCG
  - lay members may sit on only one PCG board
  - the place is open to any lay person living in the area; members of local authorities or community health councils are eligible
  - lay members holding other public positions represent the community and not other public bodies
  - the place is not open to GPs, practising nurses, non-executive directors of NHS organisations, employees of the NHS or of the DoH

- **Co-opted members**
  - anyone with specialist skills to assist the delivery of the board's responsibilities may be co-opted to the board as an associate, non-voting member
  - they will not be paid as a board member but may be remunerated under individual arrangements if the board wishes

- **Appointments**
  - the processes for nominating and appointing members must be open, fair and transparent
  - appointments will normally be for no less than one year and no more than three years

- **Meetings**
  - meetings of the board will be quorate with one third of the members (including the chair) present
  - if GPs have decided to be in the majority, a meeting will be quorate if a majority of those present are GPs
  - the meeting must be quorate for decisions and votes to be valid

> – meetings of the board should be in public; subcommittees need not meet in public but their proceedings must be transparent
>
> • **Equal opportunities**
>   – health authorities should ensure, wherever possible, that boards meet government targets for the participation of women (50%) and ethnic minorities (7%)

services). All groups will have responsibilities in all these functions; the determination of the level at which groups operated in 1999/ 2000 depended on the responsibility for commissioning taken on. Because of the redefinition of Level 3 groups as primary care trusts, and the absence (until later in 1999) of the legislation required to establish trusts, the only choice lay between Level 1 (advising the health authority on commissioning) and Level 2 (accepting the budget and commissioning responsibility for some services). This was a matter of some importance as the level of remuneration of board members is higher for Level 2 groups. The committment of the government to promote primary care trust status as quickly as possible is vivid in the requirements of groups to attain Level 2 status in 1999/2000 and the following year. After discounting health authority management costs and the commissioning of specialist services, in April 1999 groups had to take on 40% of the unified budget – roughly equivalent to prescribing costs, primary care infrastructure and the commissioning budget for community health services. From April 2000, the definition of Level 2 requires 60% of the unified budget to be delegated to the group – equivalent to the above plus all routine elective hospital care. The extensive guidance also clarifies which responsibilities of health authorities may be delegated to PCGs and which may not.

Health improvement

Working with other organisations, and utilising existing skills in public health and health promotion, PCGs will play an important role in responding directly to community health problems (Box 5.5).

Box 5.5   Some examples of the roles of PCGs in health improvement and the continuing role of health authorities

- **PCGs may**
  - give special attention to those in greatest need, for example by working with local authorities and other agencies to help drug and alcohol misusers to gain employment and face up to their addiction problems
  - work with housing agencies to reduce falls in the elderly
  - work with schools to reduce smoking and drug use
  - use community development to improve the health and health-care of disadvantaged people in some housing estates
  - ensure services for vulnerable people are more responsive to needs
  - provide individual health promotion and prevention (e.g. smoking cessation, lifestyle advice) and extend them to service initiatives such as healthy living centres
  - commission services focused on local health needs (using epidemiology, cost-effectiveness analysis, users' views, voluntary organisations)
  - assess the need for healthcare and reflect it in their primary care investment plans

- **Health authorities will**
  - retain responsibility and leadership for an effective, coordinated, multidisciplinary public health function
  - lead and coordinate comprehensive health surveillance and health protection programmes in communicable and non-communicable diseases
  - work with local authorities and other agencies to protect the public from environmental hazards
  - oversee the commissioning of important public health clinical services such as screening programmes, the protection from and treatment of HIV/AIDS, specialist services for infection control

The division of responsibilities is based on the government's judgement of an acceptable level of risk against the benefits of service integration. Public health services are a very high-risk area for politicians and have been the subject of increasing centralisation in recent years (especially national screening programmes for cancer). These are areas where failure of services will fall directly at the government's door and therefore delegation would be high risk. Contrast this with services and needs which are distinctly local in nature and where both the needs and the responsibility will remain local; the risk to politicians may be high in a very local context but not more widely. Furthermore, the probability that sensitive local responses will be made is increased by PCG arrangements, in which case the government could take the credit.

Developing primary and community health services

The primary aim is to develop and disseminate best practice in primary and community care, supported by clinical governance and by new incentive arrangements. Lead professionals must be appointed in each group for clinical governance (see above) and also for education and training, professional development and workforce planning. The task is monumental; workforce structure in primary care is uniquely complex and difficult to control and influence; the means of funding and influencing the education and training of the workforce is a mystery to almost everyone in the NHS; the impact PCGs can exert is very limited.

The quality agenda is to be supported by work published by the National Primary Care Research and Development Centre (*Quality Assessment in General Practice: supporting clinical governance in primary care groups*; accessible on the Internet on http:// www.npcrdc.man.ac.uk). Specific tasks are proposed for the group's professional lead on clinical governance (Box 5.6) and are expected to be mirrored in each practice and other partner organisations in the group.

The costs of developing clinical governance in PCGs are included in their unified budgets and, though included in the set-up costs for PCGs, are excluded from management costs.

> **Box 5.6   Responsibilities of the PCG clinical governance lead**
>
> - define a programme and a timetable where specific action will be taken
>
> - define information needs to conduct audits and reviews (including standards to measure quality and changes effected through clinical governance)
>
> - agree clinical audits (including those which cross service boundaries) with participants
>
> - ensure action is taken to improve care and to improve the knowledge, skills and attitudes of carers
>
> - ensure there is a mechanism for reporting clinical governance objectives and results

Prescribing management is at the heart of the benefits anticipated from PCGs. The unification of services through integrated provision and commissioning provides an opportunity to remove perverse incentives in the location of prescribing responsibility and to iron out inappropriate variations created by the internal market or by practitioner behaviour. Health authority action on prescribing, supported by the incentives of the fundholding scheme, have reduced variations and led to savings in prescribing costs in many areas. They remain, however, the fastest-growing component of NHS costs and their control is crucial to the overall success of the new structures. Existing mechanisms, such as Area Prescribing Committees, will remain in place but are subject to joint review by health authorities and their PCGs. Professional advice on prescribing will continue to be provided at national level, by the National Prescribing Centre, and by regional drug and therapeutics centres. Health authorities and PCGs will retain and develop local prescribing advisers, increasingly based close to practices and helping groups to make the most of the incentive schemes available.

Three-year Primary Care Investment Plans (PCIPs) were to be developed by each PCG during 1999, covering the full range of resources available to the group. As groups were in the earliest stages of their development, the timescale and ambition of these plans were moderated. However, PCIPs are central to the integration of care and the development of corporate working by PCGs. Indeed, the maturity of the group, and its ability to address a wide and complex agenda, can be effectively judged by the extent to which their PCIP deals with the main agenda of reducing health inequalities and improving health and healthcare overall. A fully developed PCIP will have a wide range of content (Box 5.7) and the group should be able to define how it will impact on the health of the population served by the group.

Box 5.7 The content of Primary Care Investment Plans

- baseline requirement for practice infrastructure for GMS, e.g. staffing and IT maintenance

- existing commitments to premises and IT costs, etc., which remain the responsibility of health authorities

- plans for additional GMS investment, including priorities and aspirations not yet agreed

- proposals for new investment in GMS infrastructure to be funded from funds held by health authorities (e.g. out-of-hours development fund)

- a stock-take of community and secondary care services currently based in practices under previous arrangements and plans for any new services

- a review of workforce issues in practices in the group

- proposals for the development of nursing services in practices and in the community

- proposals for the use of accrued savings from the previous fundholding scheme

- the proposed incentive scheme to operate in the group (the national prescribing incentive scheme in 1999/2000; an extended scheme and the use of savings from the previous year from 2000/01 onwards)

- the use of the Modernisation Fund to meet targets
- plans for CPD
- proposals for new investment in practices' staff, premises and computers
- how financial flexibility is to be used to support existing services or to reshape primary care and community services to improve health

Commissioning hospital and community services

The government's proposals for The New NHS include the replacement of the annual contracts of the internal market with service agreements and the development of long-term service agreements, joint commissioning of specialised services at a regional or sub-regional level and the abolition of the extra-contractual referral for NHS providers. In addition, the exercise of these new responsibilities will be substantially delegated over time to PCGs/trusts. To achieve this, groups will require a clear understanding of the skills and specialist advice they require, the information relevant to the commissioning of a service, the national guidance on quality standards and specialised services, and the development of risk management strategies.

PCGs will not take on the commissioning of designated specialised services; similarly, some services covering a number of groups may be commissioned in a collaborative way between a number of groups and one or more health authorities. However, all service agreements, no matter how they are arrived at, will require the approval of PCG representatives from 1999 onwards.

Although not mandatory in principle, groups must demonstrate their ability to be safe and competent commissioners of hospital services in order to ascend the scale of group status on the road to becoming a primary care trust. The gradual delegation of commissioning responsibilities had to take into account both the ending of

> **Box 5.8   Potential commissioning frameworks for PCGs**
>
> - The health authority and PCGs work together to commission services collaboratively, pooling resources to commission population-based services such as screening services and multiagency services such as palliative care
>
> - Each PCG directly commissions services used by their population, such as emergency hospital services and specialist community services
>
> - Localities or practices may, as part of a PCG, commission locally sensitive services such as practice-based community services

fundholding (with the transfer of these responsibilities to health authorities) and the build up of commissioning capacity and responsibility for PCGs. In particular, groups must show that they understand their responsibility to follow national guidance and service framworks and that they maintain service stability. They can therefore organise commissioning frameworks at three levels (Box 5.8).

It will be the responsibility of PCGs to move towards long-term service agreements. The December guidance came up with the customary banality of two long-term service agreements, one in a national priority area and one local. The pointlessness of this type of mandate is beyond belief.

To help PCGs develop quickly and with reduced risk, health authorities and NHS trusts were pressed to reduce and eliminate their financial deficits so that groups could begin without inherited financial problems. The extent to which this was achieved was variable; in most cases, remaining deficits were borne by NHS trusts and usually concealed.

Incentives

Central to the chances of success of the PCG philosophy are the incentives available to encourage changes in practice. The underlying principles of incentives in the NHS are that they should

---

Box 5.9   Underpinning principles of the PCG incentive scheme

- reward groups and practices which take on greater responsibility in a clinical and cost-effective manner

- align clinical and financial accountability

- reward high-quality care, effective practice and best value, not surpluses generated at the expense of patient care (contrary to fundholding savings from reduced hospital activity)

- integrated with clinical governance

- balance between group and practice-level reward

- attractive to health professionals and group members so there is motivation to perform well

- reward good practices in poorly performing groups

- reward year-on-year improvement in practices

- encourage good performers to help poorer performers

---

reward improvements in patient care and health outcome, they are linked to clinical governance and that they should avoid creating perverse behaviour. The 'scheme' of incentives should be simple to operate and understand, and reward acceptance of responsibility, high-quality care and the best use of resources. The full range of principles is shown in Box 5.9.

The framework for PCG incentives covers health improvement, developing primary care within practices, clinical effectiveness, and resource management at practice level within the overall framework of commissioning and the HImP. A scheme similar to the national incentive scheme for prescribing for non-fundholding practices will operate for all practices; PCGs operating at Level 2 or above may extend the scheme to commissioning. For the scheme to work effectively, high-quality practice-level data are required; where such data are not available or not sufficiently reliable, the services concerned should not be included in the scheme. Successful practices – those that operate within the constraints of

> ## Box 5.10 Rules for expenditure of savings from prescribing or commissioning in PCGs
>
> - no money can contribute directly to practice income
>
> - incentive surpluses may **not** be spent on the purchase of land or premises, hospital services, drugs, services and equipment unconnected with healthcare, any existing staff costs, to pay off loans or on practice premises investment not consistent with the PCIP
>
> - incentive surpluses may be used to purchase computers, health education materials, equipment to improve the comfort and convenience of patients and for the investigation and treatment of patients in the practice
>
> - they may also be used to pay dieticians and counsellors, non-recurring staff costs and to invest in practice premises consistent with the PCIP

the HImP, PCIP, NSFs, national priorities and clinical governance protocol yet still manage to generate surpluses – may share their surpluses with the PCG. However, surpluses resulting from windfalls will not be available to the practice. The annual deployment of surpluses at practice level is to be capped at £45 000; this ceiling may be lowered for smaller practices. Normally, practices will expect to retain the first £10 000 of surpluses and 50% of the next £70 000. The PCG will receive 50% of practice-level surpluses between £10 000 and £80 000 and 100% of any higher surpluses. Needless to say, there are also rules on how the surpluses generated may be spent (Box 5.10).

All practice spending plans in excess of £10 000 must be approved by the PCG and such expenditure must be included in the group's PCIP. Surpluses retained by the practice must be spent within two years and may not be spent at all until the practice's out-turn position for the year in which the surplus was generated has been confirmed. If the PCG overall is overspending, its share of practice surpluses must be used first to reduce/eliminate the overspend, but the practice may retain its share. Any practice may donate unspent surpluses to the group.

Managing prescribing budgets

Within the overall risk management and incentive scheme arrangements there is a specific framework for the determination of practice prescribing budgets, the shared management of risk and the incorporation of prescribing management into the incentive scheme for both PCGs and individual practices. In general, previous arrangements for the setting of budgets by health authorities, led by their prescribing advisers, is retained and delegation of this responsibility will be tightly controlled. The underlying principles of prescribing management and allocation are described in Box 5.11. A further adjustment, up to 1% of the total prescribing budget, will be retained for the development of nurse prescribing, both in practices and in community trusts; these will be integrated in primary care trusts in due course.

Work is in hand to better understand the nature of practice lists and the basis of prescribing experience. The major concern is that the sum of practice list numbers exceeds estimates and censuses of the population. To achieve the goal of basing the NHS on primary care trusts, it will be necessary to have confidence in the population

---

Box 5.11   The objectives of prescribing budgeting and the setting of budgets

- **Objectives will be**
  - fair and adequate prescribing budgets to meet the needs of patients
  - improving the cost- and clinical-effectiveness of prescribing
  - a transparent approach with the opportunity for practices to comment (but not to challenge the budget)

- **Budgets will initially be based on**
  - previous allocation with a basic uplift (inflation plus growth)
  - addition for practices with below-average budgets for the locality
  - adjustment for practices undergoing significant change
  - adjustment for significantly underspending practices (partly to avoid windfall surpluses)

figures for practices. Furthermore, the moves towards fair shares allocation of resources for hospital and community health services are to be extended to primary care and a robust and reliable population base is required to do this securely.

Towards primary care trusts

In advance of the anticipated legislation, Health Minister John Denham outlined the agenda for developing and governing primary care trusts in a letter to chairs of health authorities, PCGs and NHS trusts in February 1999. The undeveloped ideas included in *The New NHS* have been matured into a clear structure for future organisations which will form the cornerstone of the NHS for at least a decade. The benefits of primary care trusts (Box 5.12) are based on the principles described in Part 2, namely aligning clinical and financial responsibility, collective management in primary care and the delegation of decision making to local but responsible groups.

By far the most important element of primary care trusts,

Box 5.12   The benefits of primary care trusts

- better support to general practices which are the cornerstone of the NHS and of patient care

- better support to help individual clinicians in providing more effective care to patients

- better and more integration of services, particularly between general practice and community services

- creating better and fairer access to all health services, identifying for example where more locally based services need to be developed

- moving decision making closer to patients, shaped increasingly by the health professionals who most often meet their health needs

compared with fundholding, is the collectivism. Indeed, it is precisely the collective approach to primary care development which is so revolutionary, breaching the traditional secrecy which has surrounded the business of general practices. This is a remarkably intelligent means of encouraging the dismemberment of the independence of general practice, building on the noises from younger practitioners that they would not find the ending of independent practitioner status exceptionally unwelcome. While the BMA, and its time-warped grandees, will doubtless resist all the way, without bothering to consult the views of its membership, the tide has finally turned on general practice as a private sector enterprise. It may take another generation to see the end of the 1948 deal on general practice but, in contrast to many other unexpected moves by the Blair government in favour of privatisation, nationalisation of general medical practice is now on a roll.

Power, responsibility and accountability

John Denham's letter paradoxically uses language from *Working for Patients* to describe the freedoms hoped for primary care trusts. He also refers to budgets of at least £60 million, which would assume a population served of about 100 000. Assuming this is a lower limit, it reflects an average of about 150 000 while most rational observers believe that 250 000 is consistent with the powers of primary care trusts and the associated risks. It also has to be recognised that the establishment of a large number of quangos is politically risky for a government which was elected on a manifesto of quango destruction, although Margaret Thatcher had electoral success in the same scenario.

The powers of primary care trusts are essentially those to be delegated by health authorities and, for Level 4, community trusts. However, their flexibilities include facilities that do not currently exist for any NHS body. These include designing their own incentive arrangements, modernising healthcare (including practice) premises, and physically integrating primary and community care facilities. It is also intended to use the legislation to facilitate joint working between the NHS and local authorities;

> **Box 5.13 The four key principles of governance for primary care trusts**
>
> - primary care professionals, especially doctors and nurses, in the driving seat in shaping local health services
> - accountable to the health authority and subject to public accountability and financial management requirements
> - firmly rooted in the local community and responsive to local people's health needs and wishes
> - robust safeguards in place to ensure the proper use of public funds and also to prevent conflicts of professional interests from influencing the use of funds

primary care trusts will be the most likely base for the use of these new opportunities.

More important, perhaps, than power, are the responsibilities of primary care trusts, reflected in principles of governance (Box 5.13) and their continued line accountability to health authorities. Compared with PCGs, where there is reconciliation of these principles by clinical leadership in the group and wider accountability of the health authority, these elements are integrated in primary care trusts as freestanding, legally established bodies with a lay majority board (Box 5.14).

> **Box 5.14 Governance arrangements for primary care trusts**
>
> - **Structure of the board**
>   - chairman – appointed by the Secretary of State
>   - five lay members, who may include local authority elected members – appointed by the Secretary of State
>   - chief executive – appointed by the chair and lay members
>   - finance director – appointed by the chair, lay members and chief executive
>   - three professional members drawn for the executive, including

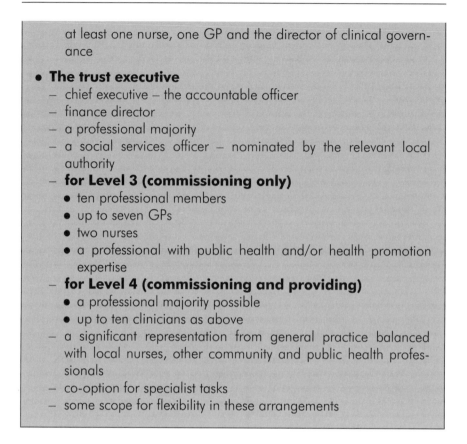

at least one nurse, one GP and the director of clinical governance

- **The trust executive**
  - chief executive – the accountable officer
  - finance director
  - a professional majority
  - a social services officer – nominated by the relevant local authority
  - **for Level 3 (commissioning only)**
    - ten professional members
    - up to seven GPs
    - two nurses
    - a professional with public health and/or health promotion expertise
  - **for Level 4 (commissioning and providing)**
    - a professional majority possible
    - up to ten clinicians as above
  - a significant representation from general practice balanced with local nurses, other community and public health professionals
  - co-option for specialist tasks
  - some scope for flexibility in these arrangements

The trust executive will carry out all the detailed work of the trust, leading the board through thinking on priorities, service policies and investment plans, and taking forward their decisions. Through the use of co-option of specialists and project teams, the executive will shape commissioning policy, primary care development and clinical governance.

The chairman and the board will be accountable to the health authority for the overall performance of the trust. While the board and the executive will have to work closely together, the board will have to reserve some decisions to itself to preserve probity. These reserved decisions will cover the remuneration of executive members, expenditure on GMS infrastructure and establishing schemes and services under the Primary Care Act.

Speed is everything

In general, NHS managers like little better than a full throttle reorganisation and the setting up of new organisations. Primary care trusts provide one of the most innovative and exciting opportunities in recent years and it is reasonable to expect a high level of enthusiasm and commitment to the endeavour. However, by giving the health professionals so much influence, the government seeks the necessary ownership of the new structures while running the risk of having the professions walk away from the whole idea. After a very high level of initial interest in primary care trusts, the profession's grandees reacted negatively to the lay majority proposed for the trust board, although no other structure was ever likely.

To achieve the scale and radicalism of change desired, the government requires an early and substantial take up of the primary care trust option. Even after seven years and a great deal of market pressure, almost half of all practices had avoided becoming fundholders. Such a level of disinterest or resistance cannot and will not be accepted. However, by giving PCGs a near guarantee of GP chairmanship and leadership, the profession has to be persuaded that its interests can be served by becoming trusts. Furthermore, the small scale of PCGs and the inevitability of larger trusts means that many leaders of groups will be relatively disfranchised under trust structures.

It will consequently fall to health authorities and to PCG chief executives to drive forward the creation of primary care trusts. The incentives to do so, and the selling point for professional representatives, must be in the level of investment in primary care and, possibly, in the direct rewards for practices and practitioners. The alternative strategy of engineering, or responding opportunistically to, a recruitment crisis in primary care seems unlikely to materialise in most of the country. Politically, it is imperative that the first wave of primary care trusts, commencing in April 2000, are successful not only in the eyes of radical reformers but also in the interests of the professions and especially general medical practice. Herein lies the principal risk to this government's entire strategy for reforming the NHS.

Further and further

Even more radical proposals are in the minds of the visionaries, dismissive of the risks incurred. For example, advocates of both integration and delegation are already speaking openly about the development of Level 5 primary care trusts, which will be providers of social services too. Level 6 primary care trusts may also be proposed, which also integrate specialist housing for people with special needs (disability or to reduce inequalities). For now, at least, service integration through the auspices of primary care trusts is definitely the political favourite.

With increasing complexity of service integration, larger organisations are likely to reduce the risks. As providers of health services, with increasing size, primary care trusts may have to develop separate units of provision for localities or specialisation (mental health, community hospitals, community services).

Part 6

The future for the National Health Service

The legislation

The 1998/99 parliamentary session proved a busy and important one for health. As well as the Health Bill, designed to effect the changes in *The New NHS* requiring primary legislation, many other legislative changes were introduced which will have a major impact on the operation of the health and social care system. This will be by far the busiest session for health throughout this parliament.

The Health Bill introduces the changes in the law necessary to implement the government's proposals. These include some technical issues, such as the formal abolition of fundholding, and some key developments in statutory functions and agencies (Box 6.1). The proposals are among the most radical ever implemented and significantly change the role and status of the key professions through the development of clinical governance and the establishment of the CHI. Developing primary care trusts may well prove to be the most radical and telling change of all, although there is no guarantee that they will deliver the outcomes desired by the

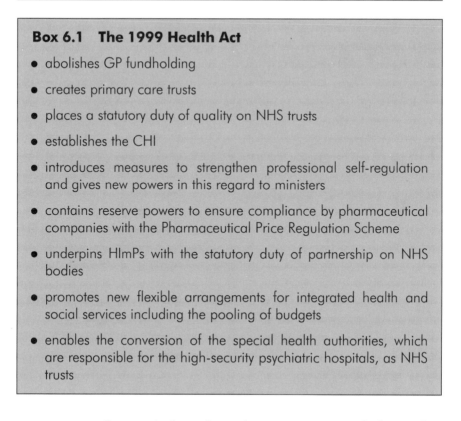

Box 6.1   The 1999 Health Act

- abolishes GP fundholding

- creates primary care trusts

- places a statutory duty of quality on NHS trusts

- establishes the CHI

- introduces measures to strengthen professional self-regulation and gives new powers in this regard to ministers

- contains reserve powers to ensure compliance by pharmaceutical companies with the Pharmaceutical Price Regulation Scheme

- underpins HImPs with the statutory duty of partnership on NHS bodies

- promotes new flexible arrangements for integrated health and social services including the pooling of budgets

- enables the conversion of the special health authorities, which are responsible for the high-security psychiatric hospitals, as NHS trusts

government. In particular, there is no reason to believe that primary care trusts will reduce NHS expenditure or prevent its frequent financial problems.

The Act introduces changes to the legal status of NHS trusts to enable the PFI to operate with the transfer of assets to the private sector partners. It also removes the statutory basis and requirement for Joint Consultative Committees and takes forward the ideas introduced in the Green Paper *Partnership in Action*. Measures are introduced to tighten up on the prevention of fraud against the NHS by family health service practitioners.

Many other legislative changes will have a direct or indirect impact on the NHS (Box 6.2). This enormous legislative programme will take the rest of the parliament to implement; its impact may not be fully realised for some years.

While the financial benefits of the Road Traffic Act will be most welcome to the NHS, adding approximately £0.5 million to the

Box 6.2   The wider legislative programme in 1998/99

- The Road Traffic Act (NHS Charges) Act
  - transfers responsibility for collecting NHS charges to a centralised agency
  - introduces a simple national tariff to reflect the real costs of treatment
  - provides for the money collected (an increase of over £100 million per year) to be transferred directly to the hospitals providing care

- The Welfare Reform Act
  - introduces a range of changes to welfare benefits and rights which can be used to help reduce inequalities in health

- Local Government (Best Value and Capping) Act
  - important legislation which puts best value on a statutory basis, replacing compulsory competitive tendering
  - Best Value requires local authorities to review all their services over a five-year period, set demanding targets for improvement, introduce audit and inspection to ensure public confidence in services

- The Greater London Authority Act
  - creating a mayor and assembly for London
  - the recreation of a Greater London Authority has led to a redrawing of the boundaries of NHS Executive Regional Offices throughout the south of England, including the establishment of a London Regional Office

- The Food Standards Agency
  - this on/off proposal from the manifesto has risks in implementation and non-implementation; it is at least something which government can do to improve food safety without it necessarily having the desired outcome

average general hospital's income, the changes to local government could well have a longer-lasting impact on public services as a whole. Something like Best Value will emerge for the NHS over time, as will the focus on stronger management rather than stronger democracy. The restructuring of the NHS Executive in response to regional assembly boundaries is a crucial symbolic act, commencing the long-term integration of public services on a regional basis.

Cynic's corner

Here is the first of two alternative endings to this analysis of the government's changes to the NHS. It is the least generous possible interpretation of events and should not be regarded as true or even as the author's most jaundiced opinion. However, it is a plausible scenario and a democratic nation must always be alert to the erosion of its freedoms and values.

The underlying tenet of cynic's corner is that everything that has occurred in the NHS since the 1997 election, and probably for some years prior to that, has been driven by the personal agendas of the Health Ministers concerned. None of the changes and initiatives imposed on the NHS in recent years had any real chance of signifi-cantly changing things for the better; their only merit was sympto-matic treatment of an unmanageable political problem – the NHS – without pitching the government of the day into the highly risky turmoil of changing the system of providing and funding health-care in the UK, towards a semi or wholly privatised service. The overriding criterion was the avoidance of risk to the future wellbeing of politicians' careers – an exercise carried out with startling incompetence – and the needs and desires of the public came low down on the list.

There may well have been occasions when political ambition and public interest accidentally coincided but, in general, politicians have told the public what they needed in terms of their latest risk-avoidance gimmick. Thus, in recent times, the political commitment to reduce waiting lists – resulting from a lone manifesto commit-ment in 1997 – has received massive resources (£310 million in England in 1998/99; almost £600 million in 1999/2000), but poten-tially more important initiatives for people's health such as cancer services, quality of care initiatives and mental health have received relatively small sums of money with many strings attached and under tight central control. Similarly, the political obsession with the risks posed by mentally ill people contrasts with the tolerance of violence and abuse caused by alcohol, a factor within the control of the culprits (unlike severe mental illness). This constitutes institutional discrimination against mentally ill people by the government.

Politicians have swamped the NHS with a wide range of initiatives to further their own interests but without any real interest in improving the NHS or meeting the needs of patients. There have been so many initiatives that many of them make no sense at all, others conflict with each other and, frankly, no one cares any more because the service is utterly exhausted by the whole initiative game. Politicians increasingly demand that everything done by NHS professionals is based on sound evidence, yet their own actions have moved further and further away from anything reminiscent of the findings of reliable research. Instead, they have fallen into the trap of their predecessors that any action initiated by politicians is right and any criticism of their actions is wrong. This is the attitude of dictators. Eventually, in the absence of effective opposition, governments stop caring about whether their actions are defensible. Increasingly, in such circumstances, their actions become indefensible.

As the panacea to the insoluble problems faced by an under-invested health service, the government has decided to develop a theme first used by its predecessor, the primary care-led NHS. It claims that the decision-making processes and financial management will be improved by delegating responsibility to PCGs, a completely untested model of management with control in the hands of people (GPs) who do not even work for the NHS. Cynics would suggest that the focus of responsibility on PCGs is a means of delegating blame as far away from the government as possible.

Thus, we have a situation in which the government is imposing frenetic changes and initiatives on an exhausted staff, and the public is being encouraged to demand higher standards and greater volumes from the NHS and accept nothing less than immortality. While investing more money in the NHS, most of the additional resources have been pre-committed by the government, precipitating a financial crisis; by demanding 3% per annum efficiency from the NHS, and depriving it of the means of generating such savings (bed closures and reduced staff), the government has rendered the NHS unmanageable. The government will blame the NHS itself for the situation which it has created.

Idealist's corner

However, here is an alternative ending, one which the government would prefer to be remembered for. After decades of self-interest by NHS professions, the government is determined to change the culture of the NHS and to shake both its staff and the public out of their complacency. The strategy consists of raising public expectations of their health service and of the health professions by making key information available direct to the public and by diluting the power of the medical profession by relatively strengthening the power of other professions, and especially nursing. New structures and accountability arrangements are required to do this and the mystique of medicine is dented by the cleverly orchestrated demonstrations of fallibility and lack of accountability by leading doctors. The government watches intently while the profession squirms and is forced to adopt a self-critical stance.

The primary drivers for change are empowerment of the people through information, weakening of the professions through the statutory duty of quality, delegation of decision making through PCGs and the role of lay members, nurses and social services within them, and the release of huge resources through a drive for greater efficiency based on comparisons. Independently, each of these drivers is a powerful force which the old guard would eventually see off; together they form an irresistible force which society demands will lead to radical and irreversible change.

The government, far from being the architect of these changes, merely creates the environment in which existing cultural changes taking place in society can be brought together to exert a major influence on an area of life (the NHS) where radical change is necessary but continuous political interference has achieved little over the years. Fundamental to the achievement of these changes is the shift of power away from the professions and towards the public. This will not happen overnight; it may take 20 years or more but it will happen, as we have seen in the USA. Indeed, the empowerment of the public is an irresistible force and, once unleashed, cannot be controlled by the government or anybody else. Nonetheless, the government regards this as a risk worth taking in order to stimulate cultural change.

Is there a case for the development of PCGs? If the intention is to integrate the various sectors of health and social care, there is no other framework that could succeed. All community-based services should work together and primary care is the generator for home-based care. General practice has to not only participate but to own this framework for it to succeed. If the intention is to manage resources better and to generate savings by much greater efficiency, then primary care is a good starting point, partly because fundholders have shown how to do it and partly because GPs are best placed to see where savings can be made in the whole system. The long-term prospect of replacing independent general medical practitioners with an employed service is probably necessary to deliver the comprehensive quality improvements sought in primary care. To play a long game and to give lead roles to primary care in the meantime suggests a high degree of shrewdness by the government.

The avalanche of initiatives imposed by the government is a regrettable but necessary symbol of their commitment to succeed with the NHS where so many others have failed. There is so much to do after the years of perceived neglect and the chaos of the collapsing market that such a scale and speed of change is inevitable and necessary. The government's demand for a very high level of efficiency gain is also part of a strategy to ensure that radical change has to be delivered. Gentleness and traditional incrementalism will not deliver the scale of change required; only unprecedented toughness and commitment to success will deliver. This explains the government's commitment to reduce waiting lists, despite professional opposition and the diversion of resources it entails. It may also explain the appointment of a tough old hand like Frank Dobson to the least popular job in government. Success breeds success and the government has been able to demonstrate early that it can deliver the apparently impossible, in terms of reducing waiting lists, by targeting resources and tight managerial accountability.

Taking the example of NHS Direct, one can see how a simple,

costly and often derided and gimmicky initiative can be a poten-
tially revolutionary force for change in the NHS. It is not so much
the existence of the 24-hour call service or the advice delivered by
nurses over the phone which is the pulsating driver for change, it is
the extended applications to which the basic technology can be put.
Using the infrastructure in the ways described in Box 6.3, NHS
Direct can be the stimulus to a permanent change in the culture of
care in the NHS, a radical restructuring of the ownership, shape
and delivery of general medical practice and a modern way of
integrating the interface between patients and services.

Although the early NHS Direct schemes were based on small
areas and delivered mainly through ambulance services, there is no
reason why this should persist as the model. Indeed, as the roll-out
of NHS Direct is completed at the end of 2000, a single and
national service (probably under a special health authority like the
National Blood Authority) can be established with no hiding place
for those who want nothing to change. Thus, the so-called gimmick
of NHS Direct can conceivably become the flagship of culture
change in The New NHS.

By accepting that radical change will take time, and the government has given itself ten years, there is a chance that this strategy

---

Box 6.3   Potential applications of NHS Direct

- a single portal of entry to all emergency healthcare services
  - '999' ambulance services
  - primary care out-of-hours services
  - social services emergency duty teams
  - communication with Accident and Emergency units

- pre-operative assessment of patients by phone or, later, video-
  phone

- post-discharge monitoring of patients for surgical recovery or
  community care packages by telephone

- surveys of user and carer experience by telephone

- delivery and reinforcement of health promotion, such as smoking
  cessation, by phone calls and messages

will succeed – at least in part. Perhaps, therefore, we stand on the threshold of the most important revolution in the history of the NHS. By empowering the people, the government is creating an entirely new environment in our society, one which it will apply to all public services. For the first time since its creation, true democracy (government of the people, for the people, by the people) will operate in the NHS.

NHS finance

The current situation

Despite the hopes and expectations of NHS staff, and the publicity surrounding the CSR and the apparently huge additional investment in the NHS, it is clear that times will be hard for the NHS in the next few years, as they have been for most of its history. Those factors which contribute to the financial difficulties of the NHS include: basic lack of funds; unfunded inflation, especially pay; rising public and professional expectations; pre-emption of funds by government; and the growth of technology and new drugs. While the first of these would be an unfair accusation against the present regime, all the others apply and will continue to impose hardship on planners and professional staff during the period covered by the National Priorities Guidance and the CSR (1999–2002).

The handling of the Modernisation Fund, including the double counting of existing recurrent expenditure, shows that there is an awareness in government of the difficulties they have placed the NHS in by fixing allocations three years ahead. Far from providing security of funding and enabling long-term financial planning, the three-year agreement on funding is acting as a straightjacket on the NHS, limiting future options in the face of inflationary pressures and rising demand. Contrary to earlier promises, and to all expectations, the government has now decided not to issue resource allocations to health authorities for the second and third years of the period of the CSR. There may well be technical reasons for this, but it also slackens slightly the shackles on medium-term NHS funding. Once the figures are announced, they become a fixed point and harder to change. By holding their fire for now, the government keeps open the possibility of changing its hard line on funding in the approach to the next election.

With the demand for 3% efficiency per year, the government has possibly set the NHS on the road to financial ruin. The calculations for 1999/2000 appear to assume that the 3% will be released in the form of cash; this may not be the intention explicitly but it is the inevitable consequence of the way the calculations have been made in order for the unavoidable funding and service pressures to be met. The government requires the NHS to deliver this level of savings each year for the three years of the programme. This exceeds the highest level of savings ever achieved by the NHS and it must be achieved without closing beds or wards or cutting staff. This is completely impossible.

It is reasonable to assume that the government has no desire to reduce the NHS to such straits and that its prospects will be improved by action on funding and efficiency in the foreseeable future. However, a lot of rules will have to be changed to enable this to come to pass. It is clear that government demands and expectations of the NHS will continue at a high level and that the NHS will increasingly bemoan its difficulties. Nonetheless, healthcare is too politically important for failure to be permitted and additional funding is the usual medicine.

The general scene

Healthcare costs are rising throughout the world. The rise in the UK has been lower and slower than in many comparable countries but it has still been sufficient to embarrass successive governments. The reasons for rising costs are extensive (Box 6.4) and are unlikely to be reversed by government action or any other event.

While most governments in the developed world struggle to limit the pace of growth in healthcare costs, the battle appears destined to be lost regardless of the endeavour, commitment, pain endured and friends lost. The record in the UK is as good as anywhere and is attributed mainly to the near monopoly of the government-funded NHS and the use of cash limits and general

---

Box 6.4   The causes of rising health costs

- ageing of the population

- advancing medical and pharmaceutical technology

- prolonged survival of people with chronic disease

- rising public expectations for advanced treatments

- reducing ageism and sexism in healthcare

- increasing standards in professional practice

- rising real costs through pay and price inflation

- long-term survival of children with severe disability

---

management to control expenditure. No other system in the world has come as close to financial balance during the last two decades. The problem for the UK is that almost all the growth in healthcare costs is borne by the NHS, the private sector being unusually small and focused on the niche market of elective surgery. If healthcare costs continue to rise, as they undoubtedly will, the issue is whether the costs will be met from general taxation in the usual way the NHS is funded or whether an alternative funding system is adopted, such as mutual insurance or co-payments, a system where patients pay for part of the cost of their care. Successive investigations into NHS funding have continually reported that the existing funding mechanism is the most economic for both the government and the country as a whole. However, the changes introduced in the Health Act to impose charges on insurance companies for the treatment of people injured in road traffic accidents is a significant step in transferring the burden of health-care costs to industry. This could be regarded as the beginnings of privatising NHS funding through the back door.

The medium-term prospect for funding

In the White Paper, the government rejects the notion that the funding of the NHS is so compromised that fundamental and visible change in the system of funding is necessary. This is not to suggest that more money is not required; it assumes both that resources can be released from existing services by improving efficiency and that the funding deficiency is at worst modest and manageable with steady annual increases. The government has committed itself to increase funding each year through the CSR and its initial actions, prior to its conclusion, were consistent with a more generous outlook for the NHS than its recent history, unexpected bonuses being delivered at regular intervals, albeit for specific purposes. Public sector finances overall in the UK are in a better state now than for a decade, with the probability of a budget surplus at the end of the millennium. Affordable growth in NHS funding over the medium term should be adequate to keep it relatively secure and enable significant improvements in services, especially waiting time reductions. However, there is a genuine risk of much of this increase being swallowed up in pay rises for staff, including lower-paid staff, if the level of the minimum wage rises significantly above the £3.60 per hour starting point.

The longer-term funding scenario

The global healthcare funding crisis will continue unabated for the foreseeable future. It is possible, but unlikely, that the existing funding mechanisms can continue for the foreseeable future. It is more likely that all the existing trends in costs will continue to rise with increasing speed and the health systems in most countries will either collapse or bankrupt the governments. In the UK, such a catastrophe is less likely as relative expenditure is low and the gap between income and expenditure is marginal – the current crisis is based on a shortfall of approximately 1% of revenue. Nonetheless, the pressures experienced by the NHS during recent years are more than likely to recur and future governments may well build on the initial attempts of the present administration and seek alternative solutions to the obvious one: spending a greater proportion of tax income on healthcare.

The government's eventual response to the report of the Royal Commission on long-term care could well hold the key to the future of the welfare state. Security and financial comfort in old age is vital to the future of our ageing and increasingly disabled population. At the lower end of the age range, more success in education holds the key to improving health under the age of 65. In older people, reduction in poverty is vital to maintaining health. Both lie at the heart of the government's overarching strategy to deal with social exclusion. Success in this venture would do more for health than increasing expenditure on the NHS.

The basic problem is that expenditure on healthcare, focused as it is on children, older people and people with chronic disability, is largely unproductive in crude economic terms. Therefore, regardless of the means of paying for healthcare (general taxation, insurance, co-payments, self-paying), expenditure on healthcare operates as a 'tax' on the productive economy.

Allocation and distribution

Since regional health authorities were abolished, NHS resources have been allocated direct to district health authorities. These allocations, and those before them to regional and district health authorities since 1977, have been based on moving towards target allocations based on fair shares of the total budget. The formula on which these targets are based changes from time to time, usually in keeping with the political priorities of the day. Thus, changes in the formula have been used to protect teaching hospitals, to protect London, to protect all inner cities and to compensate rural areas. The current formula is based on a combination of census variables which together allow for a standardised utilisation of services of equal efficiency. Recent changes have given more resources to the most deprived areas. This redistribution will focus not only on the funds for hospital and community health services, which have been the only funds affected by earlier formulae, but on the funding of prescribing and support costs in primary care, especially GMS. The maldistribution of these resources is at least twice as inequitable as those for hospitals and will lead to a significant shift away from the best-resourced areas which tend to be rural and/or affluent. The government has announced that the new formula will not be changed for three years in order to ensure a degree of financial stability for PCGs.

Now that PCGs have been established, allocations will be based on their populations, although the needs factors still relate to health authorities who will receive the funding as the statutory body to which PCGs are accountable and of which they are a part. It will be for health authorities to decide how and whether to earmark resources for specific sectors of the service and to decide the speed with which PCGs move towards their share of the target allocation. This allocation responsibility will be one of the main levers that health authorities will have to exert over PCGs and a key tool in reducing inequalities. When primary care trusts are established, these relationships will change.

Politics, medicine and the media

At least since the first appearance on television of the fictional Dr Kildare from the USA and Dr Finlay from Scotland, the viewing public has had a loving obsession for doctors and doctoring. Building on the fictional and quaint, an epidemic of realistic dramas (*Casualty*, *ER*) and 'fly-on-the-wall' documentaries (*Jimmy's*, *Children's Hospital*, *Hospital Watch*) has assaulted our television screens, usually with very high-quality productions, serving an important purpose in educating and informing the public and also helping to shape public opinion about the NHS and healthcare in general. The written media have also become alert to the massive public interest in health issues, developing both features and paper-specific styles and policies with regard to health. The basic truth is that health sells papers and attracts television audiences; truthful presentations of the issues and life in the health service fascinate, but accusations and scare stories, where truth is an optional extra, also sell. The World Wide Web is experiencing the same sort of over-exposure with an avalanche of unauthenticated policies, procedures and protocols swamping the wires and a huge amount of quasi-advertising material directed at the American audience. The focus of almost all this interest began with acute hospitals, the more technological the better. Recently, however, there has been a subtle shift in both focus and attitude. A high proportion of both news and Internet publicity involves alternative therapies and anti-technology stances. Increasingly, the media are enjoying the prospect of criticising doctors, attacking the profession in general and apparently with the at least tacit support of the government.

Politically, the medical profession has always proved a powerful force to reckon with. Governments have tangled with the collective strength of doctors at their peril and the popular support for doctors inevitably made such entanglements politically damaging or at least risky. Now, however, the government in Britain has overwhelming political power through its electoral success and enduring popularity. It also encounters a medical profession rocked by exposures of incompetence, cover up, isolated cases of alleged mass murder and a public increasingly sceptical about the magic of medicine. The opportunity for the government to achieve a degree of success in its dealings with the profession has never been greater. So what would the government like to do?

The British government's primary interest in health is with the performance, economy and acceptability of the NHS. The role of the medical profession is central to the success of the NHS; indeed, it is arguable that the only point in organising healthcare in the way we do is to bring into apposition the skills of doctors and the needs of patients. Therefore, manipulation of the NHS requires the imposition of change on the behaviours of doctors. These changes are invariably resisted, hence the continuous tension that exists between politics and medicine. It is possible that the current crisis of confidence in medicine will pass and that a loving reconciliation between doctors and the public will be celebrated. It is also possible that the present difficulties signal the beginning of an irreversible decline in the status and belief that doctors enjoy. Many of the government's subtle shifts in power bases, such as the enhanced role for nurses in PCGs, contribute to a possible negative status effect for doctors. This may help the government to exert control over the medical profession in its pursuit of a better and more flexible NHS, but a weakened medical profession will weaken, not strengthen, the NHS.

Overall, it is clear that the government has to engage with doctors to deliver its aspirations and its measures do seek to re-empower them following the experiences of the internal market and the abolition of fundholding. Governments eventually find themselves in a paradoxical double bind: they need a strong medical profession to deliver a health service they can boast of politically but they need a profession sufficiently weakened to respond to the government's bidding.

The government is now facing renewed opposition and criticism from the medical profession. Such criticism is not new but it is being reported more widely and given greater credence than during the first two years of this parliament (1997–99) due to a cooling of the love affair between the public/media and Tony Blair's administration. The relatively poor showing by the Labour Party in 1999 elections for the new National Assembly/Parliament in Wales and Scotland and for the European Parliament is symptomatic of this cooling off.

Painful reality

The government has dug a deep hole for itself during 1999. Its greatest errors might yet prove to be the NATO bombing of Yugoslavia, a risky judgement of the effects of gunboat diplomacy against a modern dictator, the failure of the Northern Ireland peace process or simple electoral complacency. Its undermining of NHS finances and capability is of a much lesser impact on the global scale of things but, to British citizens, is, perhaps, a more enduring crime.

The underlying problem is that the government is behaving like the owner of a private company, as opposed to the chairman of a public company. That is, it defines what the managers must deliver in a directive way (the political imperatives) but without accepting the responsibility for the consequences (in terms of service failures – always the fault of managers and professionals) and with a long list of incompatible rules about what must not be done (closures and job losses) in pursuit of the owners' demands. When the government lines up its promises and achievements in the run up to the next general election, in 2001, it will refer to the very limited manifesto committments on health – a reduction in waiting lists, appointing a Minister for Public Health, action on tobacco control and primary care-led commissioning. There will be nothing about HImPs or clinical governance, NSFs or primary care trusts, NHS

Direct or the CSR because these were post-election inventions. Indeed, I would expect the government to focus on the future not the past. By that time, I suspect that the NHS will be structurally insolvent in a grander manner than ever before and that it will be impossible to conceal the deficits in the way that it was under the previous regime. Some quality broadsheets are already spilling the beans on NHS funding but the government popularity balloon has not yet completely burst and the absence of a credible alternative government suggests that it will survive beyond the next election. Thereafter, however, public sector crises will return to the agenda with a vengeance.

There is much to admire in the government's strategy for the NHS. Its focus on partnership and joined-up policy is crucial; the integration of health and social services strategy, commissioning and services is long overdue; the public health leadership is very welcome; the approach to national standards is generally acknowledged to be necessary. The concentration of the government on high-level outcomes is appropriate but the complete delegation of the means of achievement while preventing effective action for political reasons is a strategy certain to implode. Particularly troubling is the reliance of the government on a catalogue of gimmicky projects in the absence of any real understanding of the need to build up the capacity of the NHS to implement both its policies and its pet projects. The high hopes of 1998 have been replaced by anger and despair at the fudge, half-truths and occasional lies. The rhetoric, especially on the level of new funding and on the freedoms of PCGs, is a long way from the reality, and the anger this causes within the NHS is rising strongly.

Governments can survive making a mess of the NHS; Labour governments probably enjoy a degree of immunity so far as the NHS is concerned. The future of the government's political success will largely depend on economic, social and military outcomes rather than healthcare; the real question is what political outcome the NHS community would like. The near universal desire for change in 1997 is gradually being replaced by mounting cynicism that no government really cares twopence about the daily personal strains and stresses which, in their millions, make up what we regard as the survival and success of our national health service.

Appendix A: Modernising Health and Social Services: National Priorities Guidance 1999/2000 to 2001/02

Published in September 1998, the National Priorities Guidance broke new ground in public sector policy making and implementation by issuing priorities for three years and by combining the priorities for health and social services. The guidance builds

---

Box A.1 National priorities for health and social services (drawn from the whole of the government's modernisation programme)

- **Social services lead**
  - children's welfare
  - inter-agency working
  - regulation

- **Shared lead**
  - cutting health inequalities
  - mental health
  - promoting independence

- **NHS lead**
  - waiting lists/times
  - primary care
  - coronary heart disease
  - cancer

systematically upon previous publications referred to earlier in this book. There are ten national priorities, with a mixture of NHS-led, social services-led and shared-led (Box A.1). The objectives for each of these ten priorities are outlined in Box A.2.

Box A.2   Objectives of the national priorities

- **Children's welfare**

To promote and safeguard the welfare of socially excluded children, and particularly of children looked after by local authorities
  - reduce to no more than 16% in all authorities, by 2001, the proportion of children looked after who have three or more placements in one year
  - improve the educational attainment of children looked after, by increasing to at least 50% by 2001 the proportion of children leaving care at 16 or later with a GCSE or GNVQ qualification; and to 75% by 2003
  - reduce by 10%, by 2002, the proportion of children who are re-registered on the child protection register (baseline 1996/97)
  - demonstrate that the level of employment, training or education among young people aged 19 in 2001/02, who were looked after by local authorities in their 17th year in 1999, is at least 60% of the level among all young people of the same age in their area
  - ensure that, within the framework of the Children Act, every

child or young person entering the public care has a comprehensive health assessment using the child's own personal child health record and developing a personal health plan with the child

- **Inter-agency working**

To improve the extent and quality of cooperative work between different public agencies with responsibilities to support looked-after children, children in need and other children at risk of exclusion

- for the three programmes which the government has introduced to help achieve these improvements (establishing youth offending teams, the crime reduction strategy and sure start partnerships), health and social services authorities working together should identify in 1999/2000 at least one significant initiative related to each of these programmes. They should also develop further initiatives in the later years

- **Regulation**

To ensure through regulatory powers and duties that adults and children in regulated services are protected from harm and from poor care standards

(pending new legislation on independent arrangements for regulation as outlined in *Modernising Social Services*)

- meet all requirements for minimum frequency of inspection
- put in place effective working arrangements for cooperation and information sharing in regulatory functions, in particular joint standards and joint inspections for dually registered homes
- carry out effective investigations into complaints regarding registered homes, particularly where there is an allegation of abuse
- have systems in place to ensure openness in the management of regulatory functions, including published standards, written policies on follow-up and enforcement procedures, and arrangements for public access to inspection reports

- **Cutting health inequalities**

To improve the health of the worst off in society at a faster rate than the rest of the population

- develop action programmes, which have measurable outcomes and are based on a shared analysis of data, to address areas of particular local health inequality, for example to reduce unwanted pregnancies, ensure services are available to, and accessible by, deprived or socially excluded groups, ensure fair access to services for black and ethnic minority groups. Local targets should be developed as part of HImPs.
- make progress towards achieving the proposed *Our Healthier Nation* target of reducing the rate of accidents by 20% by 2010, from a baseline at 1996, concentrating on children, young people and older people
- set local targets for preventing and reducing smoking prevalence to reflect the policies set out in *Smoking Kills*. In particular, health authorities should provide access to local smoking cessation services, especially for disadvantaged groups
- improve the provision of effective drug treatment and care services by working through Drug Action Teams to achieve the targets set out in *Tackling Drugs to Build a Better Britain*. In addition, improve the uptake of hepatitis B vaccination among drug users
- maintain at, or as soon as possible raise to 95%, the health authority's immunisation coverage of childhood vaccinations at age 2, basing measurement of achievement on the coverage rates for diphtheria and MMR vaccines

• **Mental health**

To improve the mental health of the population, and improve treatment and care of those with mental health problems through the provision of a comprehensive range of high-quality, effective and responsive services

- improve users' and carers' access to services, the quality of continuing care and treatment they receive, and in line with the proposed *Our Healthier Nation* target reduce the risk of suicide, by beginning to plan the implementation of the NSF
- improve the delivery of appropriate care and treatment to patients discharged from hospital by reducing nationally the

emergency psychiatric readmission rate by 2% from the 1997/ 98 baseline by 2002

- improve provision of appropriate, high-quality care and treatment for children and young people by building up locally based child and adolescent mental health services. Users of the service should be able to expect a comprehensive assessment and plan for treatment without a prolonged wait; a range of advice, consultation and care within primary care and local authority settings; a range of treatments within specialist settings based on the best evidence of effectiveness; inpatient care in a specialist setting, appropriate to their age and clinical need

- improve access to relevant mental health services and increase public safety by setting up mechanisms to support regional specialised commissioning of high and medium secure psychiatric services in shadow form by 1 April 1999 and fully by 1 April 2000

• Promoting independence
To ensure the provision of services which help adults achieve and sustain the maximum independence in their lives, including, for those of working age, their capacity to take up, remain in or return to, employment

- reduce the risk of loss of independence following unplanned and avoidable admission to hospital by reducing nationally the per capita rate of growth in emergency admissions of people aged over 75 to an annual average of 3% over the five years up to 2002/3

- prevent or delay loss of independence by developing and targeting a range of preventive services for adults, including respite care. Put in place a jointly agreed action plan

- provide carers with the support and services to maintain their health, and with the information they will need on the health status and medication of the person they are caring for. As a first step ensure that systems are in place in primary care and social services to identify patients and service users who are or who have carers

- improve older people's opportunities for optimal reccuperation and rehabilitation by implementing the proposals in *Better*

Services for Vulnerable People: maintaining the momentum

● **Waiting lists and times**

To meet the public's expectations for faster and more convenient access to modern and dependable services by reducing NHS waiting lists and times

- contribute to the achievement of the government's commitment to reduce NHS waiting lists by 100 000 from the position it inherited and deliver a consequential reduction in average waiting times
- improve the dependability of care and reduce the uncertainty of waiting, by increasing the proportion of day-case patients offered a booked date for treatment
- ensure the delivery of the 18-month maximum waiting time guarantee for admission to hospital for all patients
- ensure appropriate investment in outpatient and other ambulatory care services to work towards reducing the time patients wait for first outpatient appointments
- pilot the most effective ways of reducing waiting times in A & E departments

● **Primary care**

To develop primary and community services, in order to address inequality, improve the quality and convenience of services and increase efficiency

- ensure that each PCG has a rolling annual programme of action covering its three main functions (improving health and cutting health inequalities, commissioning services, developing primary and community services), so that by 2002 all PCG/ trusts are delivering measurable improvements against their locally agreed milestones and targets for each function
- take action and set targets with PCGs to achieve more equal access for patients to high-quality standards of general practice in terms of clinical care, speed and convenience, and the range of integrated services available close to home. Such action must include developing prompt, convenient and accessible one-stop care centres and by contributing to the national target of improving 1000 GP premises over the next three

years. It should also involve connecting all computerised GP practices to NHSnet by 1999, computerising all GP practices by 2002, and coordinating the work of NHS Direct and out-of-hours services

- reduce inequalities in access to NHS dentistry and take steps to improve oral health to be on course by 2002 to meet the 2003 national target that, on average, 5-year olds will have only one decayed, missing or filled tooth, and that 70% will have no caries at all

- take action to improve the cost and clinical effectiveness of prescribing and set local targets so that there is an increase in the level of generic prescribing, a reduction in the level of antibiotic prescribing, and progress against the cost-effectiveness prescribing measures set out in the NFAP

● Coronary heart disease
To reduce the death rate from heart disease and provide high-quality, cost-effective and responsive services for the prevention and treatment of coronary heart disease

- plan for the achievement of the proposed *Our Healthier Nation* target through the implementation of the NSF. This will include putting in place robust mechanisms for inter-agency working to ensure that joint plans covering both treatment and prevention are included in the HImPs by December 1999 for the period beginning April 2000. These plans will include targets for primary prevention; better detection of those at risk of, or with early, coronary heart disease; speedier access to emergency care; coronary revascularisation services; cardiac rehabilitation

● Cancer
To improve the quality and effectiveness of, and speed of access to, cancer services (icluding prevention, breast and cervical cancer screening, and palliative care)

- develop an integrated strategy at local level covering prevention, treatment and the modernisation of cancer services infrastructure to achieve the proposed *Our Healthier Nation* target

- reduce mortality from breast and cervical cancer by delivering the agreed national standards for each screening programme; in particular to achieve the national screening interval target for breast screening (three-yearly screening) by end March 2000; and to reduce delays in access to colposcopy services

- ensure everyone with suspected cancer will be able to see a specialist within two weeks of their GP deciding they need to be seen urgently and requesting an appointment; for all patients with suspected breast cancer by April 1999 and for all other cases of suspected cancer by 2000
- improve the quality of cancer and palliative care services by implementing the evidence-based, site-specific guidance on breast, colorectal and lung cancer; and preparing to implement similar guidelines for gynaecological and upper gastrointestinal cancers, to be published in 1999
- improve the evaluation of cancer treatment by ensuring that all NHS trusts have Service Level Agreements in place to guarantee the timely submission of complete data to their Cancer Registry

Appendix B: Highlights from the public health White Paper, *Saving Lives: Our Healthier Nation*

Unlike the Green Paper, *Saving Lives* enjoys a foreword from the Prime Minister and is signed by (mainly junior) ministers from ten departments other than health, including HM Treasury.

It reiterates the need for partnership between government, communities and individuals, starts to address public misconceptions about the level of risk (many resulting from government policy) and builds on earlier work about environmental hazards and the health impact of policy across the full range of government.

There is a broadening of government action on priority areas (Box B.1), including forthcoming supplementary strategies. Other initiatives include the Health Development Agency (Box B.2), a public health workforce strategy (Box B.3), public health observatories (Box B.4), and the public health development fund (Box B.5).

Various supplementary initiatives are promised including a

Box B.1   Targets for the national priorities

Cancer

- Reduce the total number of deaths from cancer in people aged under 75 by 20% between 1997 (69 000 per annum) and 2010 (target of 55 000 per annum) with a 2005 milestone of a reduction to 61 000 deaths per annum

- Over the period to have reduced total cancer deaths in this age group by 100 000

Cardiovascular disease and stroke

- Reduce the total number of deaths from cardiovascular disease and stroke in people aged under 75 by 40% between 1997 (69 000 per annum) and 2010 (target of 41 000 per annum) with a 2005 milestone of 51 500 deaths per annum

- Over the period to have reduced total cardiovascular disease and stroke deaths in this age group by 200 000

Accidents

- Reduce the total number of deaths from accidents in people under 75 by 20% between 1997 (10 000 per annum) and 2010 (target of 8000 per annum) with a 2005 milestone of 8800 deaths per annum

- Over the period to have reduced total accidental deaths in this age group by 12 000

- In addition, to have secured a reduction of 10% in the number of serious injuries resulting from accidents

Suicide

- Reduce the total number of deaths from suicide by 20% between 1997 (4500 per annum) and 2010 (target of 3600 per annum) with a 2005 milestone of 4000 deaths per annum

- Over the period to have reduced deaths from suicide by 4000

Monitoring progress

The government will publish every three years a national review of life expectancy, health experience and health inequalities

sexual health strategy, seeking a 50% reduction in pregnancies under the age of 18 by 2010, and a new national strategy for the fight against HIV and AIDS. In the field of drug misuse, the national strategy, *Tackling Drugs to Build a Better Britain*, a shift in action and resources is envisaged away from the consequences of drugs (mainly expenditure on criminal justice) towards the prevention of drug misuse and the treatment of people affected by drugs. A national strategy for alcohol is also promised. The long promised and much argued over Food Standards Agency is to be set up soon and the Chief Medical Officer is to lead a strategy to reduce illness and death from communicable diseases. The government has commissioned the Centre for Reviews and Dissemination at the University of York to update the evidence base on the benefits and risks of fluoridation of the water supply to prevent dental disease. If this review confirms the safety and effectiveness of fluoridation, the government will legislate to impose a legal obligation on water companies to add fluoride to drinking water if local people request it. The responsibility for ascertaining local views will transfer from health authorities to local authorities. Finally, the government is establishing a Human Genetics Commission to advise on how the advances in genetic knowledge and technology can be applied safely to promote health and prevent disease.

The Health Development Agency will replace the Health Education Authority and will inherit its chairman and non-executive directors. However, set up as a Special Health Authority and with a much wider set of responsibilities, the HDA sounds more like a National Institute for Public Health Excellence.

The agency will be set up using existing resources invested in the activities of the Health Education Authority and the Department of Health and, subject to legislation, will be operative from January 2000.

The public health workforce has been dominated by doctors for 150 years. Recently, health authorities have effectively utilised

Box B.2   Roles and responsibilities of the proposed Health Development Agency

- To map the evidence for action to improve the public health and health improvement

- Commission research and evaluation to strengthen the evidence base for programmes to improve health and reduce inequalities in health

- Advise on evidence-based standards for public health and health promotion and on their implementation

- Advise on the successful targeting of health promotion measures on the worst off in order to narrow the health gap

- Disseminate guidance on effective practice to public health and health promotion professionals

- Commission and conduct evidence-based national health promotion programmes, integrated with work being done by the DoH

- Advise on the capacity and capability of the public health workforce

many other staff with specialist skills but neither their training nor their career structures are formalised and they are unable to achieve the most senior posts. A new workforce strategy is required.

Box B.3   A public health workforce strategy

- There is a need for truly multidisciplinary public health

- Proper training programmes and career structures will be developed for non-medical public health professionals; a public health workforce national development plan will be promulgated to ensure these are in place

- The national development plan will be informed by a public health skills audit

- The new public health workforce will have a bigger role for nurses and the public health practitioner role of health visitors and school nurses will be reinvented

- A post of specialist in public health, of equivalent status to consultant in public health medicine, will be created for non-medical public health professionals

- Regulations will be changed to enable non-medical public health specialists to become directors of public health

- A pilot of medical care epidemiologists working with providers in the Northern and Yorkshire region will be extended to the whole country and to PCGs

A system for improving health monitoring and measurement will be introduced at regional level, based on the public health observatory developed in Liverpool in 1990. In addition to a core set of measurements, the government will encourage the development of disease registers in some places, building on the value and use of universal cancer registration. It is also intended that annual reports of the director of public health will be used more systematically.

Box B.4 A public health observatory in each region to...

- monitor health trends

- identify gaps in health information

- advise on health and health inequalities impact assessments

- integrate information sources across agencies which describe health and health needs

- carry out projects to highlight certain issues

- evaluate local progress on improving health and reducing inequalities

- scan for future real or potential public health problems

They will be subject to a common set of standards, will provide the health basis for HImPs and will be written in ways which make them relevant to the role of local authorities in health improvement.

The government will ensure the development of a research and development strategy for public health, under the auspices of the Central Research and Development Committee and using resources already identified within the NHS R&D programme. To help deliver the changes outlined, the government will create a number of fast-track academic posts in public health and the Medical Research Council will join with the NHS R&D programme to create joint R&D fellowships in public health.

As ever, the ubiquitous Modernisation Fund is rediscovered to fund and promote initiatives in public health.

Box B.5   The public health development fund

- Comprising £96m from the modernisation fund over three years
- £25m will be available in the first year (1999/2000)
  - £9m will be spent on national initiatives in the four national priorities, in an infant feeding programme and to create an innovation fund for health visitors and school nurses
  - £3.5m will be used to support national initiatives on healthy settings
  - £3.5m will be used to support a national health citizens programme
  - £4m will be available to support specific initiatives in the regions, including the development of the public health functions
  - £5m will be used for other initiatives including public health observatories, work on impact assessment and the proposed improvements in infection control measures

Further reading

Audit Commission (1997) *Higher Purchase: commissioning specialised services in the NHS*. Audit Commission, London.

Department of the Environment, Transport and the Regions (1998) *A New Deal for Transport: better for everyone*. Stationery Office, London.

Department of the Environment, Transport and the Regions (1998) *Modern Local Government: in touch with the people*. Stationery Office, London.

Department of Health (1989) *Working for Patients*. HMSO, London.

Department of Health (1995) *Commissioning Cancer Services. Report of the Expert Advisory Group on Cancer*. (Calman–Hine report). Department of Health, London.

Department of Health (1997) *Health Action Zones*. Invitations to bid, EL(97)65. Stationery Office, London.

Department of Health (1998) *Information for Health: an information strategy for the modern NHS*. HSC 1998/168. Stationery Office, London.

Department of Health (1998) *Modernising Social Services*. Stationery Office, London.

Department of Health (1998) *Our Healthier Nation*. Stationery Office, London.

Department of Health (1998) *Partnership in Action*. Stationery Office, London.

Department of Health (1998) *Smoking Kills*. HSC 1998/234. Stationery Office, London.

Department of Health (1998) *Working Together: securing a quality workforce for the NHS*. HSC 1998/162. Stationery Office, London.

Department of Health (1999) *Clinical Governance: quality in the new NHS*. HSC 1999/065. Stationery Office, London.

Department of Health (1999) *Saving Lives: Our Healthier Nation*. Stationery Office, London.

NHS Executive (1998) *A First Class Service*. Consultation document on quality in the NHS, HSC 1998/113. NHSE, Leeds.

NHS Executive (1998) *Clinical Effectiveness Indicators*. HSC 1998/085. NHSE, Leeds.

NHS Executive (1998) *Health Improvement Programmes: planning for better health and better health care*. HSC 1998/167. NHSE, Leeds.

NHS Executive (1998) *Modernising Health and Social Services: National Priorities Guidance 1999/00–2001/02*. HSC 1998/159. NHSE, Leeds.

NHS Excecutive (1998) *Modernising Mental Health Services: safe, sound and supportive, a national strategy for mental health*. HSC 1998/233. NHSE, Leeds.

NHS Executive (1998) *The New NHS: commissioning specialised services*. NHSE, Leeds.

NHS Executive (1998) *The New NHS Modern and Dependable. A National Framework for Assessing Performance*. Consultation Document EL(98)4. NHSE, Leeds.

Secretary of State for Health (1997) *The New NHS: modern, dependable*. Stationery Office, London.

Primary care group guidance
HSC 1998/065 Establishing primary care groups

HSC 1998/139 Developing primary care groups

HSC 1998/140 Setting unified health authority and primary care group baselines

HSC 1998/171 Health authority and primary care group allocations

HSC 1998/179 Primary care groups: clearing house facilities

HSC 1998/190 Primary care group remuneration

HSC 1998/228 Primary care groups: delivering the agenda

HSC 1998/230 Governing arrangements for primary care groups

HSC 1999/048 Corporate governance for primary care groups

Index